Start Your Own
MEDICAL CLAIMS &
TRANSCRIPTION
Business

PRENTICE HALL PRESS

PRENTICE HALL PRESS
A member of Penguin Putnam Inc.
375 Hudson Street
New York, N.Y. 10014
www.penguinputnam.com

CIP data available.

Printed in the United States of America

15 14 13 12 11 10 9 8

ISBN 0-7352-0083-1

Most Prentice Hall Press Books are available at special quantity discounts for bulk purchases for sales promotions, premiums, fund-raising, or educational use. Special books, or book excerpts, can also be created to fit specific needs.

For details, write: Special Markets, Penguin Putnam Inc., 375 Hudson Street, New York, New York 10014.

CONTENTS

PREFACE

Start Your Own Medical Claims and Transcription Business is the result of many hours of in-depth research into one of the fastest growing opportunities in home-based business today. Our exclusive team of National Business Library's professional business writers has brought years of practical experience to this project, and we know that the information provided in this book will set you on the road to success.

Owning your own business can be the most exciting and rewarding venture you will ever experience. We talk of hundreds of small business owners who make comments like, "Doing something I really enjoy makes every day a pleasure," or "If I had known I would be realizing this kind of income, rather than making my former boss wealthy, I would have started my own business years ago."

It's true! You'll never get rich working for someone else. By capitalizing on your experience, investing time and energy, and studying the proven techniques and business methods provided in this book, you will be well on the way to realizing your goals for success in your own venture. It takes courage to begin. Without a doubt, the first step is the hardest–and you have already taken it.

INTRODUCTION:
MEDICAL MONEY MIRACLES

Are you a detail person? Have you always been blessed with the attitude that things should be done quickly, efficiently, and done right the first time? Well congratulations, you may be the perfect candidate for a career in two exciting new fields that are growing by leaps and bound, the lucrative fields of Medical Transcription and Medical Claims Processing.

Every day, in every part of the country, doctors, nurses, hospitals, and clinics are inundated with medical reports to be prepared and medical forms to be completed and processed. Every patient requires a medical history. Every illness needs a diagnosis. And every insurance company requires doctors' reports for accidents and major illnesses. For doctors and their staff to try and do this work themselves means less time that they can spend with patients—their main concern and their main source of income. So, more and more, this type of work is being farmed out to people just like you—people who like a challenge and are looking for a career that can be done at home on a part-time or full-time basis, and maybe even be expanded into a larger business away from home.

Thanks once again to the baby-boomer generation, both Medical Transcription and Medical Claims Processing are fields that are expanding rapidly and will continue to expand for years to come. As of January 1, 1996, baby boomers began turning fifty—at an alarming rate! And as you know, the older people are the more often they need to visit doctors and hospitals. And the more they visit doctors and hospitals, the more paperwork is generated.

As you will see later in this book, it is this enormous amount of paperwork that has spawned a new opportunity in Medical Claims Processing, that is processing forms by computer and sending those forms directly to insurance companies by modem. A rough estimate is that one million practitioners are practicing in the United States today. Each of these practitioners processes hundreds of insurance claims every month. Yet only about 15% of all insurance claims are being processed computer to computer. That leaves millions of claims each month to be processed by hand or to be introduced into the new computerized system. Individuals with a business capable of performing these computerized transfers will definitely be in the right place at the right time.

Medical Transcriptionists are also steadily abandoning the typewriter and turning to word processors and computers to complete reports for doctors and hospitals. Not only do they have the advantage of keeping large bulky documents safely tucked away in easy to find computer files, but they also have the advantage, as we will talk about later, of purchasing specialized computer programs that make their transcription tasks that much easier—and more profitable.

So what's the monetary opportunity associated with Medical Transcription and Medical Claims Processing? People presently employed in these fields are reporting incomes up to $25,000 annually during their first year of business. Others who have been in the business longer are reporting incomes of $40,000 per year and more. And many in this field that started out with a small, simple home-base business have seen such growth that they have opened their own offices near hospitals or doctors' offices where most of their business comes from. Some have opened offices in large medical centers that cater to older patients and generate thousands of insurance forms and medical reports every day. Others have even hired staffs and are running very profitable medium to large size concerns. Both fields seem to be limited only by how much time and effort you want to put into them—but don't forget—there's a great big world of medicine out there and they need you!

1

THE GROWTH OF SMALL BUSINESS

The 1980s were referred to as America's "entrepreneurial era." In 1986, more than 750,000 new businesses were created in the United States. In 1989, more than a million new ventures were started nationwide—almost half of them by women. In 1991, there were 20.5 million small businesses in the United States—and the entrepreneurial era is continuing through the 1990s. The recession of the early 1990s compelled suddenly unemployed people to start their own businesses in order to survive. An upsurge in part-time businesses has also fueled an entrepreneurial trend, with people in search of extra income working on profitable ventures during their off hours.

More and more people are opting to leave their 9-to-5 jobs and stop "making someone else" rich to focus their energies on building a successful business of their own. The combined circumstances of fewer advancement opportunities, lack of job security, and the possibility of retiring without a pension are also driving the trend toward self-employment.

Today, the number of individuals who are self-employed is at its highest level ever, and based on your interest in this book, it's quite possible that you'll be joining the ranks of small business owners in the near future. It may be simply a dream right now, but that's how these businesses start.

Starting and operating your own small business is one of the most exciting and satisfying challenges you can undertake. There are no limitations on income potential when you're investing time and energy in your own enterprise. With the practical information provided in this book and dedication to your business goals, your chances for success are excellent.

What Is a Small Business?

The majority of businesses in the United States today are classified as small business. The definitions of what constitutes a small business run the gamut from the size of the overall staff (typically under 100) to the amount of assets or sales volume. However, in this book, small business is defined as one that is independently owned and operated.

The major benefit of this type of business is that you have the ability to make decisions quickly and act on them immediately. What typically bogs down big business is the number of people involved in the decision-making process.

Other advantages include the fact that small businesses can provide personalized service to the community or the market they're serving and the owner has the freedom, independence, and control to operate exactly as he or she chooses.

It's important to remember, however, that most major corporations, from Ford Motor Company and McDonald's to Mary Kay Cosmetics, started out as small businesses—as dreams.

It was because of basic business sense and a willingness to learn and adapt as their companies grew that Henry Ford, Ray Kroc, and Mary Kay, and thousands like them, steered their dreams into monumental financial successes.

Whether your goal is to supplement an existing income and to operate a solely owned home-based business from your garage, kitchen table, or spare bedroom, or to start a business that involves raising substantial capital, finding and setting up a commercial location, and hiring employees, you have the potential to enjoy an independent lifestyle that carries with it a number of rewards. And the rewards are as varied as the people who pursue them.

Accepting the Challenge

Remember, these rewards do not come without hard work and the willingness to research and understand all facets of running your business. Many new businesses fail within the first few years.

Reasons given for the early demise of a small business range from lack of organization or management experience to undercapitalization, misunderstanding of the importance of advertising, inexperience in pricing products and services, lack of an overall business plan, improper hiring practices, and failure to accurately assess the competition.

It isn't that someone purposely starts a business without having explored these areas. However, many times a person feels that his or her demonstrated expertise while in the employ of another can easily be transferred into a personal business. This is only partially true.

While it is imperative that you have particular skills or talents—because selling them is what your ultimate success will be based on—it's equally important to understand how to sell them, to know exactly what your profit margin is, and what steps you need to take to ensure the continued growth of your business.

Sounds easy, right? It really can be. But like anything else worth doing, starting your own business means careful planning. For example, you wouldn't consider taking a month-long vacation without doing some serious planning to ensure that the house was taken care of while you were gone, that you had made reservations for lodging, tours, and flights, and that you had converted your cash into traveler's checks.

There are so many aspects involved in running a business, it is vital to be prepared for any eventuality. Being prepared means being informed, so that when situations do arise you know how to deal with them.

Is "Failure" Really Failure?

We have all heard stories about people who started their businesses on a shoestring and who became successful because of their sheer determination to make it work. It does happen, but these people are the exception rather than the rule, and in most cases have had experts standing behind them to give them guidance when problems came up. Others fail and, unfortunately, this often holds potential new business owners back. We hear and read about amazingly high figures related to so-called business failures.

According to a research project conducted by Albert Shapero, professor of the American Free Enterprise System at Ohio State University for many years, no one really knows the true failure rate of new businesses. The main reason for this is because there is not really a standard definition of "failure" in this case. He points out that a number of businesses close for a variety of reasons, many of which are not documented.

For example, in some cases the owners reach retirement age and have no one to pass the business along to; others shut down because the owners simply get bored; while still other entrepreneurs file a Chapter 11 bankruptcy, which basically gives them the opportunity to stay in business and continue operating under a court-approved plan, even though they become a statistic on the "failure" list.

The other extremely important aspect to consider when thinking about the benefits and risks of starting your own business is that having a business fail has never been a deterrent for true entrepreneurs. Many well-known business moguls failed at least once, and often more than once, before striking it rich.

Learning from Experience

In fact, almost anyone who has had a business fail will tell you that the experience was more valuable than anything they could have been taught in a business school, and that it provided them with the knowledge they needed to start another venture successfully. This kind of determination is a valid qualification for self-employment and will pay off handsomely.

When you own your own business, you are responsible for everything. There will be times, such as when your accounts receivable are running sixty days late or the phone company puts the wrong number in your Yellow Pages listing, when returning to the 9-to-5 world will seem like a tempting option.

This is where self-discipline, an unwavering belief in your product or service, and the determination to be your own boss will pull you through.

But, again, we can't stress enough the importance of planning, understanding basic business practices, being aware of consumer trends, and taking the time to develop, implement, and update goals to ensure success for your efforts.

What This Book Offers

This book is designed to provide you with the information you will need to start your Medical Claims and Transcription business, to offer techniques to help you with day-to-day operations, and to provide anecdotes about people just like you who had a dream and, through planning and determination, were able to turn that dream into a successful reality.

In addition to focusing on aspects of the Medical Claims and Transcription business, we cover such important business matters as:

- Recognizing the entrepreneurial profile
- Taking our exclusive Entrepreneurial Quiz
- Finding the right audience for your business through easy marketing techniques
- Organizing for efficiency
- Recognizing legalities
- Addressing financial concerns
- Getting your home office up and running
- Charting your enterprise's growth

You will find specific how-to information on

- Advertising and promoting your business
- Finding capital
- Saving money on operating expenses
- Developing a simple bookkeeping system that will show you whether you're facing a financial crisis or realizing a profit.

You're never too young, too old, too busy, or too poor to start a business. Owning your own business means taking advantage of our marvelous system of free enterprise. Earning a substantial living and, even better, realizing a profit for doing something that you enjoy is the American dream come true.

The opportunities for entrepreneurs have never been better. Armed with a solid product or service to sell, the determination to succeed and, most important, business know-how, there is nothing that can stand in your way.

Notes

Key Points:

_____

_____

_____

_____

Personal Thoughts:

_____

_____

_____

_____

_____

_____

_____

_____

_____

Additional Research:

_____

_____

_____

_____

_____

2

THE RIGHT STUFF:
THE ENTREPRENEURIAL PROFILE

Starting a business is one thing: making it work is another. We know that success in self-employment is largely the result of careful planning and understanding basic business techniques and formulas.

It is equally important that you start a business based on your expertise in a specific field and focused on your involvement in an area that you thoroughly enjoy. As many successful entrepreneurs claim, making money doing something you love is the best way to ensure a profitable future. It is always easier to address the inevitable business challenges that crop up when you are, at bottom line, creating a product or providing a service that gives you a sense of pleasure and personal satisfaction.

Personality is also a factor in determining what kind of business to get involved in, the way you will eventually set up the legal structure (sole proprietorship, partnership, etc.) and how you will run the business on a day-to-day basis. For example, if you are planning to start a business that is based on your artistic or creative abilities, it is possible that your personality is not suited to the very important aspect of sales. But without strong selling abilities there is a likelihood that your goal of distributing, for example, your hand-carved wooden boxes nationally will not come to fruition.

This isn't to say that you should decide against going into business for yourself. It simply indicates it would be in your best interest to join forces with someone who does have strong selling skills, who believes in the product as much as you do and will work toward a common goal.

On the other hand, if your personality is geared to working with people, it is a good idea to consider a business that will emphasize this ability, such as developing seminars or workshops based on your area of expertise, providing independent counseling or tutoring, or a service such as gift basket designing, which depends on your interaction with people on a one-to-one or on a group basis for success.

Self-motivation, otherwise known as drive, is one of the most important personality traits of successful entrepreneurs. This is the characteristic that gets you going and keeps you moving when you are in business for yourself. It's what helps you to keep turning out those craft items, upgrading your technical skills or developing new and improved promotional techniques when business is slow. It's what gives you the tenacity and confidence to call on a potential client even though they have told you "No" three times.

Self-motivation is also what helps you overcome the fears and concerns that inevitably arise when you own your own business. It is the main ingredient that has spurred on those people we hear about who have achieved success despite drawbacks, such as minimal capital, lack of education or limited experience.

People with a high degree of self-motivation see the greatest obstacles, such as learning a new aspect of business management, as a new and exciting challenge to overcome. If you've ever undertaken a project without fully understanding the mechanics involved in performing the task or knowing what the outcome would be, you were operating on self-motivation—the conviction that you would be able to learn whatever needed to be done to accomplish your goal.

And regardless of the outcome of the project, you undoubtedly gained more experience and knowledge than you had before, which only works to increase your sense of motivation to handle new challenges.

Research shows that the true entrepreneur should possess the following kinds of personality traits in order to be able to address the many and varied situations that arise in business ownership:

Ten Traits of Successful Entrepreneurs

1. **Motivation**
(Self-driven, goal-oriented)

2. **Confidence**
(Belief in oneself & one's goals)

3. **Self-Awareness**
(Cognizance of one's positives & negatives)

4. **Courage**
(What separates the entrepreneur from the dreamer)

5. **Curiosity**
(The constant need to increase awareness)

6. **Optimism**
(Expectant, forward-looking)

7. **Flexibility**
(Adaptable to changing needs)

8. **Decisiveness**
(Able to make quick, wise decisions)

9. **Patience**
(With people as well as circumstances)

10. **Drive**
(The unquenchable desire to succeed)

The willingness to take risks. Courage is a valuable trait when striving for success. We have heard successful people say something similar to this: "I don't know how I did it; I just made a phone call and asked for the money I needed." It was more than luck that made it possible for this person to raise the capital they needed to get their business off the ground; it was the willingness to take a chance—in this case, the risk that they would receive a positive response to the request.

The owner of a small cabinet-refinishing business said, "I always figure that the worst thing that can happen is someone will say no, so it never hurts to try." In the game of business, you must be willing to take chances. Even if you don't get exactly what you want every time, the odds are good that if you feel strongly about what you need, you will get it. But you have to ask!

Confidence. The age-old philosophy of positive thinking is a step in the direction of success. By behaving as if you already are a success at what you do, it follows that you will be, and your customers will believe it too. A confident attitude is one of the most appealing traits you can exhibit to a prospective client, for it lets them know that they will be getting the best their money can buy.

Patience. When you own your own business, there will be moments when you feel like the roof is caving in, especially when your suppliers seem to be taking their own sweet time in fulfilling an important order or when a customer's demands seem to be unrealistic. Although you may be able to hurry the supplier along, you must remember that your customers are always right, since they are the ones who can financially make or break your business.

If you are aware that patience is not a strong suit, develop a stop-gap exercise for yourself to use at times when coping is a definite necessity. Whether its the time-honored "count to ten before saying a word" theory, visualizing a pleasant scene or repeating a secret phrase to yourself when tension is running high, it will be to your advantage.

Decision-making. Business has been described as a process of making one fast decision after another. Often, a decision has to be made immediately, on the spur of the moment. In those instances, you should go with your intuition and trust that you are doing the right thing.

However, if you are the type of person who prefers to analyze your options, weigh all the factors and make decisions slowly, then that is what you must do. It will not only keep your confidence intact, but will ensure that you're taking the right action. Again, careful planning will help you predict many of the decision-making situations arising in business. As time goes by and you grow more comfortable in your role as business owner, you'll find yourself making faster decisions.

> *You have to accept whatever comes, and the important thing is that you meet it with courage and with the best you have to give.*
>
> *Eleanor Roosevelt*

Experience. The results of a Dun & Bradstreet survey conducted a few years back indicated that a primary reason some businesses fail within a few years of start-up is "incompetence in the area of business experience." Whether or not your experience is directly related to the business you're planning to start, it's a key component for growth.

If you feel you don't have enough business experience, there are several avenues you can take before starting your own enterprise. Returning to school for specialized courses is one answer. Most community colleges and adult education facilities offer classes and seminars in business start-up and maintenance these days. There are also hundreds of courses available to you by mail—over 1,200 schools and universities now offer home study or correspondence courses which will, in many cases, give you official certification in your field.

However, your best solution is to take a job in the field you're interested in. By asking questions about all aspects of the business, you will gain experience, get paid for learning and find out whether this is really what you want to do—before sinking money, time and energy into the enterprise.

Perseverance. One of the adages you will hear time and time again when talking to entrepreneurs is that perseverance is 90 percent of the battle to succeed. If you are like the majority of new small business owners, the entire staff and support system for your venture is probably you. Making a dream come true can be a lonely task, especially when you are just getting started, and ensuring that it works often means little rest or relaxation. You must be willing to persevere during the rough times, to hang in there during the slow periods and to maintain your belief in your product and service even when it seems like no one else in the world knows you exist. It has been written that through perseverance the snail reached the ark. So it is with success!

The Entrepreneurial A-to-Z Appraisal

Owning a business calls for the ability to handle different situations with confidence. The following self-appraisal quiz has no right or wrong answers. It is designed to help you in determining personality traits, attitudes and qualifications that will benefit you in your venture.

The Entrepreneurial Quiz

Use the letter "*S*" for strong or "*N*" for needs improvement beside the characteristics listed below. Give yourself sufficient time to analyze each trait. Upon completion, use the appraisal as a starting point for discussions with friends and family members about your business profile. Acknowledging the strong and weak points will help you prepare for your role as an entrepreneur.

Achievement: I have a strong desire to be successful in my chosen business venture. _____

Belief: I have a faith in myself and the service or product I am specializing in to build my business. _____

Creativity: I am able to address situations in imaginative and innovative ways to reach my goals. _____

Discipline: I am self-motivated and able to handle necessary tasks, whether or not I enjoy them. _____

Efficient: I am organized and able to arrange my priorities or change my work methods as needed for maximum production. _____

Friendly: I am genuinely interested in people and enjoy my interactions with them on a day-to-day basis. _____

Goal-Oriented: I have a tendency to set my sights on preset goals and to work hard toward them. _____

Health-Conscious: I am aware of my physical abilities and have the insight to work smart in order to preserve my health. _____

Independent: I am able to work alone, if necessary, and prefer to be responsible for my own actions. _____

Judgment: My conclusions about people or situations are generally accurate. _____

Knowledge: I have solid experience in my field and have spent enough time in a professional business setting to learn the ropes. _____

Leadership: I am able to direct people effectively while instilling confidence and loyalty. _____

Maturity: I am willing to work toward long-term goals and do not get upset by the inevitable minor setbacks. _____

Networking: I am willing to develop associations with other entrepreneurs for bilateral support in my venture. _____

Optimism: I am able to see what is right about a situation and to explore its potential to the fullest. _____

Positive Attitude: I am convinced that I can accomplish anything I decide to do and rarely entertain negative thoughts. _____

Questioning: I am not afraid to ask questions to get the information I need to expand my knowledge. _____

Resourceful: I am able to find ways to accomplish just about any task I must do. _____

Sales Ability: I can present information about myself and/or my business in a convincing yet honest manner. _____

Tolerance: I am able to handle stressful situations with a positive and realistic attitude. _____

Undaunted Spirit: I am unafraid of the unknown. In fact, I enjoy a challenge and accept the consequences of my actions. _____

Venturesome: I am not afraid of hard work to reach my goals and enjoy finding new, positive ways to handle troublesome situations. _____

Well-balanced: I generally maintain a sense of humor when things don't work out as expected. _____

Expressive: I am able to express ideas and feelings, both orally and in written form, with clarity and logic. _____

Youthful Nature: I am capable of tackling work with enthusiasm and a high level of energy. _____

Zest: I look forward to enjoying my business, the people I will be dealing with and the resulting fruits of my labor. _____

Scoring

Although this is not a test, merely a tool to provide you with information about your entrepreneurial profile, there are immediate clues to your future as a business owner in the responses you have given.

If you have indicated 15 or more "S" codes, there is a good possibility that you have been involved in your own business in the past or, at least, have worked in a managerial capacity for someone else. You have the positive personality traits required to be a successful business owner. If you have between 8 and 15 "S" responses, you are basically a positive and directed person and should not have any problem with improving certain areas to increase your personal business success potential.

If you have fewer than 8 "S" responses, this is an indication that finding a complimentary business partner who can support your goals may be an option worth considering.

3

THE NEED FOR
MEDICAL CLAIMS & TRANSCRIPTION

As you can see in the news, the healthcare industry is growing at an alarming rate: the population is demanding more
family doctors, more psychiatrists, more specialists, more
physical therapists, even more acupuncturists. Baby-boomers
alone are causing the demand to more than double!

So what's the best way to capitalize on this trend? It
should start to become very clear. Simply put, it doesn't
matter what area you look at, one thing remains the
same—Medical Transcriptionists are needed across the
board! Podiatrists, orthodontists, gynecologists, psycholo-
gists—they all need their office, laboratory and hospital
notes, procedures and diagnoses written up into easy to
read forms.

Medical transcription is one of the fastest growing
areas of employment, according to the American Hospital
Association, and it's one of the best home-based businesses for low start-up costs and high profits. It doesn't require

much more than a good ear, a commitment to accuracy and a flair for typing. The whole business involves the simple act of typing up a doctor's dictated notes. Granted, you may be thinking that doctors use a lot of medical terms and codes you couldn't possibly know, but a good medical dictionary and computer software can solve most of these problems.

Overview of Medical Transcription

This is a labor intensive business with strong income potential and steady growth. It does not lend itself to absentee ownership and can be started from home with the owner as sole employee.

Minimum Start-up Investment:	$1,000
Average Start-up Investment:	$5,000
High Start-up Investment:	$7,500-$10,000
Breakeven Point:	Three to six months
Average Annual Gross Revenues:	$25,000-$40,000
Potential Annual Gross Revenues:	$75,000+

Times Are Changing

It used to be that transcriptionists had to use manual typewriters, carbon paper, and horribly noisy dictation machines—not to mention that if mistakes were made or something needed to be added, the whole report had to be retyped. Thankfully, personal computers and digital dictation machines have greatly simplified this business, making it a perfect low cost home business—working comfortably where and when you want.

This simplification can be seen in some of the day-to-day tasks of a medical transcription business:

- Reports can be edited on screen
- You can choose which word processing program you want to use.
- Your computer software can automatically type in common or medical term instantly as you go, along with checking your spelling and grammar.
- Each document can be easily named and saved for future reference or editing.
- You can instantly get a line or character count (vital since you will normally bill by the line count).
- You can professionally print out your finished reports, on your desktop, the second they're done, or send them electronically anywhere in the world instantly.
- Dictations are time stamped, can be instantly archived and called up for review, and your time involvement can be specifically monitored to make sure you're making the kind of money you should be.

Where to Begin

So, you feel that medical transcription is the perfect business for you to get into, but you don't know where to start. No problem. There are a number of ways to get into this business quickly and affordably, but it helps to have some of the basics already taken care of.

What You Need

It is entirely possible to teach yourself how to become a qualified medical transcriptionist at home. You may already be off to a good start if you: type over 50 words per minute; have a good "ear" for vocabulary and grammar; have your own personal computer and word processing program; and you like research. Let's take a look at each of these so you can assess your knowledge.

How are your typing skills? This is arguably the most important aspect of medical transcription. You can see that the faster you are able to type, the more work you can accomplish. There are many transcriptionists that start out only typing around 40 words per minute, but over time, it will increase dramatically the more you work. If you can't type at all, there are plenty of books, classes and even automatic software that you can get to help you learn.

How is your "ear"? Being able to recognize words you know, and correctly learn, or look up, those you don't, is the second most important aspect to this business. Many doctors' dictating styles can range from too slow to too fast, crystal clear to mumbled—not to mention that some doctors might be speaking English as a second language, making a strong accent hard to decipher.

Do you have a computer and word processing software? It doesn't really matter what type of computer (IBM, PC Clone, Macintosh) you have as long as you have a decent word processing program like WordPerfect, Microsoft Word, or AmiPro. Many medical transcriptionists are using old IBM PCs and getting the job done perfectly. Thankfully, the prices for new computers have come down dramatically and almost all now come standard with word processing programs—making it affordable if you do need to purchase these items.

What about additional equipment? A transcription machine is another vital necessity (how can you transcribe without one?). The type of machine will depend greatly on what your clients are used to using—micro or standard, digital or analog? Do some research before making the purchase. Also keep in mind that you will need a good printer. Ink jet printers are now in the $150 to $300 range and their print quality is remarkable—perfect for printing reports. And do you plan on sending transcriptions electronically? A computer modem (about $50 to $300) will be another piece of necessary equipment to add to your transcription arsenal. (The Equipment section later in this guide will get into the specifics of what's needed.)

Do you enjoy learning? As a medical transcriptionist, you will be increasing your knowledge daily, learning new words for procedures, surgeries, medications, tools, conditions, etc. A medical, standard and drug dictionary will be handy desk references for terminology that you may not know. Having a commitment to better your understanding and continually grow in this area will also guarantee your success. It will be a tough road if you only learn the bare necessities and refuse to go any further.

Even if you don't have any of these qualifications, don't despair—all of this can be remedied.

Many accredited schools offer home learning courses in medical transcription. You can learn at your own speed with all the professional materials sent directly to you—audio tapes, flash cards, easy-to-understand textbooks—with instructors simply a phone call away if you have any problems.

Or if you have the time and resources, going to school will give you one-on-one training while opening the doors for job placement once you've become qualified as a medical transcriptionist.

Do you know someone who is already a medical transcriptionist? Becoming an apprentice and learning the ropes from a qualified person who is currently working in the industry is one of the best ways to learn the finer points of the trade. They will know who to contact specifically in your area and be able to give you all sorts of "inside" information.

Medical transcription, when done correctly, can be a very satisfying source of income. So whether you learn at home, school, from a friend or teach yourself, once you understand the processes, terminology and work ethic involved, you should be able to enter the job market confident that you will be a success.

The Claims Boom

According to recent statistics over 4 billion medical insurance claims were processed nationwide in 1989. That number jumped dramatically to 6 billion in 1991 then surpassed 8 billion in 1995. Industry analysts say that we will easily see 12 billion or more in just the next few years!

The problem (for patients, doctors and the insurance companies) is that only roughly 15% of these claims are being processed electronically and without error—leaving a whopping 90% (over 7 billion) insurance claims being inaccurately processed the old-fashioned paper way.

Paper claims have become the bane of the industry by slowing processing and payments, to well over three months in most instances, due to incomplete forms, improper filing and, worst of all, blatantly wrong information. Patients are being billed for procedures that weren't performed, medications that weren't administered, or supplies that weren't used; doctors can't get operation approvals on time or drug prescriptions for patients without scrutiny. This is one of the reasons our healthcare system is in such disarray.

And this is where you come in.

In the last few years there has been a cry to arms against the spiraling costs of healthcare. The Federal Government is trying to manage the situation, but isn't having much luck. A key weapon in the war is electronic claims processing and automated patient billing. Statistics show that over 22 percent of the nation's $800-billion-a-year healthcare bill is spent on processing and paying healthcare claims alone!

Electronic claims processing and automated patient billing can save over $9 billion a year, making it one of the best cost-saving opportunities in the healthcare industry today—but best of all, those savings go directly into your pocket!

So how do you enter this money-making field? What will it require? What will your primary focus be? How much money will you ultimately make? I'm sure all these questions are swimming around in your head, so let's get started right away!

Your Role

As we've mentioned, there are two general areas that the medical claims, or billing, business covers: the provider side and the patient side. Currently both areas are growing rapidly (the baby-boomer generation is now passing 50 and we will see the largest segment of the population ever requiring healthcare and medical services) causing unheard of demand for more and more qualified medical billing people and small businesses.

What's Up, Doc?

It's the providers (doctors, healthcare facilities and hospitals) that generate almost all of the claims (or bills) for the medical industry. These claims must be filed with each patient's insurance company, (Medicare, Medicaid, Blue Cross, Blue Shield, etc.) for reimbursement of procedures performed, medicines administered, facilities utilized and other services used.

Only until recently were all claims required to be manually typed or handwritten on a paper form known as the HCFA (Health Care Financing Administration) 1500. This form, and the processing involved, accounts for most of the lag time between an insurance company's authorization and final payment to the doctor or healthcare facility for services rendered.

Thankfully, now with advancements in computer technology, almost all claims can be filled out, processed and paid electronically in a fraction of the time paper forms take.

Filing claims electronically greatly reduces errors and speeds up the entire claims process. This is a boon for doctors because it means they get paid in less than 20 days, as opposed to the three to six months paper claims can take. Medicare and most other insurance companies also prefer electronic claims because they can be processed less expensively than paper claims. In almost all cases, electronic claims get priority handling because of the reduced data entry and verification procedure time and costs. Your ability to process claims this way will be a major selling point when searching for your new clients. Being able to save a doctor or healthcare manager weeks, if not months, of time and confusion will quickly catapult you into this high profit business.

The (Patient) Patient

How many times have you heard that someone was misbilled from a doctor or healthcare provider? Drugs that weren't used, tests that weren't performed, or even hospital stays that never happened have been showing up on patient invoices for years. Which is why we need to look at the other side of the healthcare money equation: medical claims adjustment.

You may want to focus your new business in this medical claims area, performing audits for people with fairly regular healthcare needs. You become a watchdog, of sorts, keeping an eye on unscrupulous doctors, inept healthcare staff and manipulating insurance companies that will overcharge or falsely bill for things your customer never received. You get paid a percentage for every mistake you find. A medical blood test can run well over a couple hundred dollars, and finding a single misbilled item like this could net you around $50. Considering that some bills are more than 30% incorrect, you can see how just finding a handful of mistakes can bring in some real profit.

Your ability to request itemized bills and detailed procedure lists then sort through and verify each one is at the heart of this business. Being organized and having an inquisitive mind are the two main components to this rewarding opportunity.

A Full-Service Commitment

Once you're familiar with the claims process and feel comfortable that you can handle yourself in the healthcare industry, expanding into a full-service management company is a natural step.

The most profitable billing companies will do more than just take care of claims for their clients. They will also handle general billing and receivables for the healthcare provider.

For example, once you've sent in your insurance claim, the insurance company will pay the doctor directly. But, since most insurance only covers about 80 percent of any given claim, the doctor needs to bill the patient for the remaining amount. You invoice for the balance due and handle any collection problems that may be involved. You could even expand the business further by handling payroll or patient scheduling.

Most billing companies that handle claims only will charge by the claim. This averages from $3 to $5 per claim. A full-service operation, on the other hand, will generally receive a percentage of the provider's total billed invoices, which can run from 5 to 10 percent. Considering that many healthcare providers and doctors bill up to a million per year, even 5% works out to $50,000—not bad.

Know Your Stuff

No matter which area of medical claims or billing you decide to enter, the more knowledgeable you are about the industry the better. You might be able to market yourself perfectly, and get a foot in the door, but without a comfortable understanding of the processes and procedures involved, you could easily sink rather than swim.

This business guide will give you a very good overview of what's involved for all these business opportunities, but it will be up to you to further your knowledge by investigating and researching the healthcare industry. Understanding the terminology and standard modes of operation will not only give you piece of mind, but will translate into a very profitable future.

The Computer Necessity

For whichever business or businesses you decide to start, be it medical transcription, medical claims or a full-service management company, you can see the one instrument that will be vital in your success—the computer.

The medical industry, and these businesses in particular, rely heavily on computers, modems, printers and software to get the job done profitably. These items may seem overwhelming, but once you have a general understanding of your computer and its various peripherals, you will see that the software will do a majority of the work very easily and accurately—and in most cases, it will even run by itself! (For more information on outfitting your business, see the Equipment section).

4

MARKETING YOUR MEDICAL CLAIMS & TRANSCRIPTION BUSINESS

Just about every business can be divided into three parts: marketing, bookkeeping, and operations—each one completely dependent on the other. Without paying attention to all three areas, your new venture will not succeed.

A medical transcription business is no exception. Performing the actual task of typing up dictation is the operation part; billing for services, writing checks for supplies, and depositing money is the bookkeeping part; making contacts, finding clients, and selling your services are all part of marketing.

Start with the Market

How many potential transcription clients are available to you? What are they willing to pay for your services? How do you find your first clients? What type of transcription service are they used to? Even before you spend a single dollar on your new medical transcription business, you must find out the answers to all of these questions—marketing will do the job.

Doctors and healthcare providers across the board—surgeons, psychiatrists, dentists, podiatrists, etc.—all need transcriptionists. How many providers are in your area? Where's the nearest hospital? Is there a medical transcription service already operating in town? The phone book would be a simple place to start to get this information.

Do a survey by contacting these local doctors, clinics, hospitals, chiropractors, radiology laboratories, physical therapists and medical transcription services and asking them the following questions:

1. Do they have on-site transcriptionists or use outside home workers?

2. How much experience do they require?

3. What kind of dictation equipment do they use (tapes or digital)?

4. What medical dictionaries do they use?

5. Do they pick up and deliver?

6. Do they know a transcriptionist who has overflow work and might need help?

You will find from these questions that everybody's probably doing something different. They might be doing it "in-house" and are looking for an outside agency (you); they might refer you to their current agency who might be looking for transcriptionists; or you could find out what the current agency charges, enabling you to offer better pricing and service when you are ready.

Can you use any personal contacts? Do you know anyone who is a doctor or works for one? Do you have any friends or relatives who work in a clinic or hospital? The question to ask is, "How can I get into the local market as a medical transcriptionist?" Make contacts and record all the information you get.

Another approach is to find another medical transcriptionist who has too much work (this is usually the case). Many transcriptionists will not only provide you with work, but will also help you out by recommending certain equipment, explaining procedures and letting you in on some "trade secrets."

If calling isn't getting you too far, you can always make "office calls"—visiting doctors' offices and speaking to the receptionist or other office staff. You can explain that you are starting a medical transcription business and are looking for possible clients. They should be able to provide you with enough info to proceed with your new business venture.

Getting That First Client

Your initial marketing survey should have given you your go-ahead as to how, and who, to approach when you're ready to start transcribing. Once you're comfortable with your level of study, practice and understanding of medical transcription, you will want to start making money—so building a client base is your next step.

Since you're establishing a professional business, it needs to have a professional appearance. A separate phone line, business cards, and a Yellow Pages listing under the heading MEDICAL TRANSCRIPTION SERVICES or MEDICAL RECORDS are a few of the necessities that will show you are open for business.

The people you called in your survey are your first likely candidates. Call each one, or stop by to announce your transcription services are available. Leave a resume or business card (or even a brochure about your business, if you have the resources to put one together) so they will know whom to call when the need arises. You may have spoken to more than a few secretaries who are plenty tired of doing transcription—have them sell the doctor on an outside service whereby they don't have to pay insurance or benefits.

Search the newspaper under Fictitious Business Statements in the classifieds section. New medical offices and clinics are being opened all the time. Often these businesses start off slowly and on a limited budget. New providers may feel they cannot afford a medical transcriptionist since their patient base is small. You can offer to grow with them; starting at a lower rate with an agreement to increase over time, or starting at a lower rate in exchange for experience.

You don't have to limit your search for clients to physicians only. Medical, chiropractic, and nursing schools, along with physical therapists, home healthcare agencies, insurance carriers, and even attorneys need to document patient care and may not be using a medical transcriptionist at present.

If you feel you aren't getting anywhere and the phone isn't ringing, there are some more tantalizing marketing schemes you can try to at least get potential clients to give you a chance.

Some beginning transcriptionists will offer a free day, or even week of transcription services to potential clients just to show how good their services are. Or, you can offer a "buy one—get one free" deal where they get one free report for each paid transcription. These are only a couple of the many ideas that you can use to get your first clients.

Meeting the Client

Just as if you were applying for a job as an employee, having doctor's choose you for their medical transcription will take a fairly extensive interview—they need to be sure that you will operate to their expectations as far as accuracy, clarity and confidentiality go.

When meeting your first potential client it's best not to come right out and say that you have no experience (if this is the case). If you feel comfortable with your level of understanding of the business, your ability to answer the questions honestly and directly will show that you are serious about your services. You are a professional—act professionally. Highlight your abilities: training, knowledge, typing speed, and accuracy, and be able to show sample work that you've done recently. Some of the things that you should emphasize include:

1. Top quality transcription.

2. Extreme confidentiality of information.

3. Less than 48 hour turnaround on request.

4. Deadlines are never missed.

5. You have state-of-the-art equipment.

6. You have a pleasant, easy to work with manner.

If the client decides to use your services, great; if not, call and find out exactly why you weren't chosen. This will help you plan for your next client.

Some of the problems amateur transcriptionists have is not being able to learn from each setback, or feeling intimidated by the doctor. No matter how things go, always stay honest and true to yourself. It might take a few attempts, but it will happen. With the right amount of persistence, you will become a profitable medical transcriptionist.

Cementing the Deal

Once you have your first client(s) you will want to guarantee your rates, length of services and legal obligations. This will take the form of a standard contract between you and each of your clients.

Sample Contract

This contract is made and entered into on _____(date) by _____(client) located at _____ (address)

and

_____(your name or company name) located at _____(address). In consideration of the mutual promises in this contract, the parties agree to abide by all the terms of this contact.

Contractor agrees to do the following:
Medical transcription in accordance
with client's guidelines and forms.

Services shall include: _____

_____

_____

_____

Turnaround for transcription services shall be_____hours.

Pickup and delivery of the materials needed to complete this service will be the client's responsibility, or his/her appointed courier, and performed at such a time agreed to by both parties. Contractor promises that the final product will be completed to the client's satisfaction.

(If charging by the line)
For performing the work described above, client agrees to pay contractor the amount of _____ per line. It is agreed that sixty-five (65) characters constitutes a line.

(If charging by dictation time)
For performing the work described above, client agrees to pay contractor the amount of _____ per minute dictation time. It is agreed that any recorded media submitted by _____ for transcription has been checked for overall length; or digital dictation times have been recorded for verification.

Either party may terminate this agreement on not less than thirty (30) days' notice.

Confidentiality: As a contractor, it is my responsibility not to violate any confidence of the patient or their family through indiscriminate discussion pertaining to patients, their treatment, diagnosis, or progress. Erroneous and nonpublic information released by me shall result in legal liability. I understand and agree that all patient records and patient information are strictly confidential and will not make any disclosures.

Errors and Omissions Insurance: It is my policy that computer-authenticated or other artificial signatures generated by means other than the actual dictating physician's signature are not endorsed by me. Therefore, the doctors should proofread their transcription for document content, accuracy and quality control.

No changes shall be made in this agreement unless those changes are agreed to in writing by both contractor and client.

Signed _____(client)   _____(you)

Where's the Market Right Now?

There is a great shortage of transcriptionists today, mainly because of the increase in the number of doctors, patients and healthcare resources. It's a perfect time to get in on the ground floor and realize your dream of becoming an entrepreneur. But always remember: good marketing doesn't substitute for adequate experience—no matter how you present yourself, you'd better have the know-how to back it up.

The Market for Claims

Getting clients for your medical claims business will take more than just your ability to do the job—it will take marketing—the ability to convince potential clients that your service is professional and you have the ability to do their billing as well, if not better, than anyone else.

Finding your prospective client is every bit as important as being experienced, perhaps more so in medical claims. Most people find that getting their first provider is the hardest part. A key strategy is often to convince the potential client that it is better to use an outside professional billing agency than to rely on an inside staff person who usually cannot keep up with the constant changes in insurance and Medicare rules. Staff people often change and move on, too, so that by using an outside agency, the provider can count on more consistent and reliable service.

The more expert you can become in understanding the medical claims process, insurance guidelines and in working with your electronic claims software, the better your chances are to convince a provider to give you his or her accounts.

Where to Look

By doing some basic market research in your area, you will be able to assess your potential in the business. Talk to your own doctor about electronic billing—whom they use, how much they pay and what services are offered. (You can also use many of the same tactics used in the medical transcription section for finding clients.)

It's important to have a set list of benefits that your service will provide, explaining how much better off a provider will be when they come on board. If you have the ability to file claims electronically you can tout that:

- *Their insurance claims will be paid in 7 to 21 days on the average.*

  The average provider has an outstanding accounts receivable of well over $25,000. This is usually caused because of the lag time and rejection rate of paper claims, which don't get paid in less than 30 to 90 days. Filing electronically through your service will get them paid quickly—improving their cash flow dramatically.

- *You can reduce their rejected claims to an average of 2%.*

  Insurance carriers and government agencies reject an average of 20% to 25% of all paper claims submitted. This is mostly due to human error and insufficient information. Electronic Claims processing helps to ensure error free claims resulting in 98% of them being promptly paid without delay.

- *You can reduce current claims processing costs by up to 75%.*

  Processing claims electronically definitely costs the provider less than filing paper claims. The American

Medical Association stated that the average provider spends $7.00 to $15.00 processing each claim by paper, compared to $3.00 to $5.00 electronically.

- *You will free up staff time.*

  Your service can perform all phases of electronic claims processing. A healthcare provider's staff will no longer be required to file claims and make time consuming follow-up calls. Therefore, the staff's duties can be redirected to assist the practice in other areas, such as improved patient relations and acquiring new patients.

You should also note that your services can be customized to fit into your provider's time schedule and work flow—without any problem. Some offices will want you to pick up the superbills and enter the claims manually. Some may want a total billing service where you process claims, prepare patient statements, post payments, do all the follow-up and collections. Some offices may even want you to handle only the claims that have been rejected but never resubmitted. You simply design your service to meet their needs.

Lots of Opportunity

Knowing how simple electronic claims filing is, you may be wondering why more providers don't all use this system. As surprising as it might seem, only about 15% of all claims are being filed electronically! Knowing why providers aren't already using these sophisticated methods will help you plan your marketing approach:

Time is the first and foremost factor. Many doctors run into the constraints of daily patient care and the myriad office tasks that keep them too busy to even consider changing their billing procedure internally.

Some practices may have looked at electronic billing previously, but were discouraged due to cost. They don't want to consider the amount of money it would take to set up their own internal system. What they don't know is that the costs to get into electronic billing have come down dramatically in just the last couple of years.

Quite a few practices are completely aware of the benefits of electronic claims filing but are confused or intimidated by the entire computer aspect of the business. They don't know where to begin, what hardware is needed, what software is best, etc.—but you will.

The Lure of Medical Bill Auditing

Maybe you've decided to work on the patient side of medical claims and are interested in finding individuals with a high number of medical bills. This is a more intimate arrangement than dealing with a provider—you will need your potential clients to open up and divulge all their personal and medical information.

Because of this, you will want to present yourself as a very professional, personable and trustworthy service provider. You will take the time to make sure that their records, insurance data and medical charges are in order while maintaining the utmost confidentiality. These qualities should show up on your business card, resume or other correspondence material.

My Marketing List of Potential Customers

_____

_____

_____

_____

_____

_____

_____

_____

_____

_____

_____

_____

_____

_____

_____

_____

_____

_____

_____

_____

_____

_____

_____

Marketing: in General

Now that you have selected the kind of business you want to own, it is important to explore the need for it. A process called *marketing research* will provide you with the information you need to develop your business, plan methods of distribution or promotion, and set prices which are tailored to the audience you hope to attract.

In addition, your marketing research will provide you with information that will help when you are making decisions about a location, hours of operation, the specific types of services and/or products to sell and how to gear your advertising.

Identifying Your Market

The process of identifying your audience may seem to be an extremely complex process, however, you can develop a perfectly workable and valuable marketing report using the guidelines which follow and adapting them to your particular situation. Basically, there are five factors used to target the market:

Population: The number of households in the region you are considering as a target for your business is crucial as you must have a sufficient population base to produce the sales you need to generate a profit. Equally important is the circulation and age range of readers of any magazine you will be focusing your advertising on for specific products. If, for example, the readership of a particular publication is largely of retirement age, it would not fare well if you were planning to sell products for infants. It would, however, work in your favor if you were promoting health products or even gift items.

Income: Your potential customers must have the income to purchase goods and services. Consumers in the

35-65 age group generally have considerable income which they spend on household items, personal grooming and sporting goods. This is not to discount the over-65 age group, a good-size and growing segment of the nation's population which, depending on the region, will have adequate discretionary income (money after taxes and necessities) to spend, or the 18-35 age group, which would be a desirable market for clothing, personal and recreational items.

Competition: As an example, the recent influx of frozen yogurt shops in warm climate regions made it difficult for late-comers to make a dent in the market. This is almost always the case and, therefore, competition shouldn't be a negative factor. Rather, it should spur you on to stretch your creativity by coming up with something brand new or a similar product or service that is superior to those being offered by the competition—either through quality, selection or price.

Product or service market match: Basically, this means that you must be able to attract those consumers whom you have the resources to serve. As an example, if your idea of the perfect business involves national distribution of your patented weight-training equipment, you must: a) reach an audience that is receptive and interested in body building through a carefully designed advertising campaign, and b) have the financing available to supply and ship the product.

Desire: Your objective is to match your product or service to the needs and desires of a particular group of consumers who will be responsive. It is often difficult to figure out exactly what your target market wants; however, through observation of what the competition is doing, it should be possible to recognize a need.

Market Research Techniques

Large corporations often have in-house marketing staffs which conduct extensive research on a continuing basis to ensure that the products or services being offered are in line with the marketplace.

Obviously, this is an expensive and time-consuming process—one that you undoubtedly want to avoid.

Through several easy and inexpensive methods, you can find out everything you want to know about your potential market. The first step, however, is to determine exactly what information you need. It might be trends in population figures or regional economy or how many new homes were built within the last five years in your area.

The nearest Census Bureau office and your local chamber of commerce are consistently good sources for regional statistics. The reference librarian at the public library can steer you toward other local data and fact sheets which will give you the specifics you seek. Also, the Small Business Administration compiles extensive marketing information, in addition to material on operating procedures for specific types of businesses.

Check the Directory of Trade Associations at the library to find the name and address of the advisory board for your industries (or check the Resources listed at the end of this Guide). These trade boards exist to provide associates with marketing statistics, management tips and a wealth of valuable information. Often it only takes a phone call to get more details than you could ever use.

Another excellent source of information on population, income and sales figures is the annual survey of buying power published by Sales and Marketing Management agazine, which breaks the information down by county and cities in the United States and should be available through the library.

Media Kits and Personal Contact

The advertising departments of local magazines and news-papers undoubtedly have a "Media Kit" available for potential advertisers, which they will gladly send you upon request. These packets contain a breakdown of their advertising rates and specifications, a description of why advertising with them is to your benefit and, most important, a profile of their readership. A friendly conversation with one of their salespeople should give you a wealth of data.

Talking with the people you will be buying supplies, equipment and products from is another excellent source. They can give you a good run-down on trends, as well as an overview of current sales figures for their products. Since they are hoping you will eventually use them as a supplier for your business, they will be more than happy to give you free information.

It is, of course, often possible to gauge what the competition is doing and to glean information from them. There

> ### Five Factors Used in Targeting Your Market
>
> 1. Population
> 2. Income
> 3. Competition
> 4. Market Match
> 5. Desire

are two approaches when talking to people who are soon to be in direct competition. One is to be up-front and honest about your business plans and appeal to their sense of "industry spirit."

Surprisingly, you will find the direct approach works in the majority of cases as most people are genuinely interested in and supportive of others trying to make it in their field. It is better for everyone if "industry" standards are maintained and competitors have a healthy rapport. And, except in extreme situations such as a very small community, there is generally enough business to go around. It shouldn't be difficult to capture your share of the market, especially if you can develop something unique to attract them.

On the other hand, if competitors are less than receptive, it may be necessary to partake in a bit of super-sleuthing to get the information you want. A little brainstorming with friends should result in a few good ideas if you find it necessary to resort to investigative techniques.

Focus Groups

If you really want to go into depth with your marketing study, you might consider gathering together a group of people (family members, a social or church group, or friends) for a "focus" session to determine whether your product or service will match the needs of the prospective audience. This involves presenting your proposed business idea, with product samples if applicable, and creating a questionnaire that calls for specific answers from the group members.

> *The greatest thing in the world is not so much where we stand as in what direction we are moving.*
>
> *Oliver Wendell Holmes*

This method is often used by major companies when they are testing new products and, in fact, there are private companies around the nation who do nothing but put focus groups together and set up testing sites in stores, shopping malls and street corners to obtain spontaneous and objective input from potential consumers.

The questions you would want to include on your questionnaire would ideally cover such aspects as how often members of the focus group have used a similar service or product in the past, what they liked about it, what they found to be unsatisfactory, how they feel it could have been improved, whether they would be willing to try another, their age, income and any specifics that relate to your proposed business.

For medical claims or transcription business, the questions might include a breakdown of the top three reasons people in your focus group would consider using a service like yours, what type of claims or transcription they would purchase and what *additional* services they would like to see offered. This kind of information will give you an immediate edge on the competition when you are ready to start advertising.

Analyzing Your Research

The bottom line in conducting your research is that you want to zero in on information which provides insights on the potential for your business idea before you invest time, money and energy in setting it up.

If, for example, you were considering starting your business in a small community and your focus group information indicated that only 10 percent of the local residents would consider using it, you would definitely want to reconsider the validity of your concept or figure ways to promote it on a broader scale. On the other hand, if your marketing research pointed out that 90 percent of the population thought it was the greatest idea since sliced bread and that 50 percent would have an immediate need for it, the potential for your business would be much greater and proceeding with the idea would probably guarantee a profitable venture.

Buy an inexpensive notebook to help you keep track of your marketing data. Use a separate page for each category you are researching. The notebook will serve as your personal, ongoing market study to be reviewed and amended as your business grows and the audience you are serving changes.

Plan to update your information as new studies are published (generally an annual event) indicating changes in population, economy or buying and spending trends. Most newspapers publish synopses of local, state and federal studies of this nature, so maintaining your notebook shouldn't be a problem. You should also reserve several pages to record comments and suggestions from customers once your business is established, which will help you personalize the service to the market and keep you a step ahead of your competitors.

Spend as much time as needed to feel comfortable about your marketing project.

The important point is that the results of your research are comprehensive enough to provide you with concrete information on who your potential customers are and how you can best reach them.

Target audience:

_____

_____

_____

_____

Ideas for reaching the audience:

_____

_____

_____

_____

_____

_____

_____

_____

_____

Additional research information:

_____

_____

_____

_____

_____

_____

Review

- I have completed my entrepreneurial profile to determine my strengths and weaknesses. _____

- My friends and/or relatives have given me additional input based on the profile. _____

- I am aware of the advantages and disadvantages of going into business for myself. _____

- Time is not a problem; I can easily devote the time I'll need to build my business. _____

- The important people in my life are supportive of my decision. _____

- I have analyzed my personal cash flow to insure that I can support myself and my family for at least six months or until the business is solvent. _____

- I feel confident about my future as a business owner at this point. _____

- I know what people want as far as my business is concerned. _____

- I have conducted informal studies to determine my potential customers and understand their needs. _____

- I have analyzed the competition, know what they offer and have a general idea about their success ratio. _____

- I have done my marketing research and know how to get in touch with the audience I want to reach. _____

- I have contacted the trade association for my industry and have accumulated facts and figures regarding the pros and cons of starting my own business. _____

- I feel confident that my product or service is saleable. _____

Notes

_____

_____

_____

_____

_____

_____

_____

_____

_____

_____

_____

_____

_____

_____

_____

_____

_____

_____

_____

_____

5

LOCATION:
HOME OR COMMERCIAL OFFICE?

Medical claims or transcription could be an ideal enterprise to start from home. However, whether you'll be permitted to operate such a business from your home will depend on local zoning ordinances, perhaps your landlord, or other restrictions. Laws pertaining to the operation of a home business vary by county and state. It's illegal to conduct a home-based business in certain areas, while in many others across the country it's acceptable as long as local requirements are met.

The Home Office

By operating all aspects of your business from home, you'll save much-needed capital that would otherwise be spent on a commercial location. That money could go toward your all-important early-stage marketing.

If you live alone, you can basically set up your business anywhere that is comfortable for you. But if you share your living quarters with other people, it may be necessary to use a little creativity in planning an office area in a home-based business situation. A spare room, a basement or attic or family room can be turned into an office quite simply with the addition of a worktable or desk, shelving for storage and a telephone.

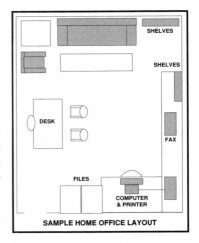

SAMPLE HOME OFFICE LAYOUT

The main consideration, once you get the business rolling, is to have a permanent base of operations so that you can leave unfinished work without disturbance and that you have a place to put supplies and business records for easy access. Do not, under any circumstances, attempt to do bookkeeping and other functions at the kitchen table or on a folding card table. You will find yourself spending countless hours having to put things away or move them somewhere else to accommodate family life.

Utilities and Phone

The home-based business has an additional advantage: Your phone line and utilities are already in place. Any additional equipment is easy to obtain from your utility carriers because you already have an established payment history.

Single-line telephone systems are adequate for most small businesses. But if your business eventually outgrows a single-line system, you'll need a multi-line system enabling you to accept several calls simultaneously and switch between lines.

Regardless of whether you need a single line or a multi-line system, some basic options are now available when choosing equipment.

Programmable memory allows automatic storage and instant dialing of phone numbers by pressing a button or entering a code.

Automatic redial reconnects the last number dialed, in some cases redialing at specific intervals until the call goes through.

Speed dialing allows you to quickly access frequently dialed numbers by using a one- to four-digit code.

Call waiting is especially useful for businesses with single lines, allowing you to take incoming calls while putting the original caller on hold.

Conference calling is often a related feature of call waiting, allowing you to simultaneously speak with two or more parties at multiple locations.

Call forwarding routes incoming calls to a pre-programmed phone number at another location.

Cordless phones are especially useful for the home business, allowing you to make or accept calls from any location in the house. Because cordless phones vary in quality, it's recommended that you thoroughly research the market before buying.

Speaker phones allow you to carry on conversations without the constraint of holding a receiver. One of the main benefits is that you can accomplish other tasks while waiting on hold. They're also useful for note-taking and similar chores during business conversations.

Voice mail is a combination answering, routing, and messaging system that can help cut front-office payroll costs while maximizing efficiency. Customers dialing a voice mail number are greeted by a recorded message and given a menu of options: direct-dialing employees in other departments; leaving messages for one or more individuals; receiving additional recorded information; and using the voice mail system with a rotary-dial phone.

The cost of voice mail has been scaled down dramatically in recent years, and is now available for small or even one-person businesses, presenting a first-class image while actually saving you money (not only in payroll costs but in avoiding potential lost revenues from unanswered or misdirected calls).

Long Distance Carriers

Whether you're a one-person home-based operation or an expanding business in a commercial location, long-distance service is, of course, essential.

With AT&T, U.S. Sprint, MCI, and a host of other carriers competing for your long-distance dollar, conflicting claims and a wide range of advertised services can leave the small-business person bewildered when trying to make a choice.

> *When deciding on a long-distance carrier, consider the areas of the country and the world you'll most frequently be calling, and the monthly amount you plan to spend.*

The maze of carriers is actually two-tiered, the upper tier consisting of the major-network providers (such as AT&T) that offer direct lines to customers, and the lower tier made up of regional and national carriers that lease their lines from the major providers.

When deciding which carrier to use for your business, consider the following: the areas of the country and the world that you will most frequently be calling; the monthly amount you anticipate spending on long-distance calls; the time of day you'll be making most of your calls; any seasonal calling patterns; and whether you'll be dealing only with clients statewide (in which case a regional WATS line would be a cost-effective choice).

In addition, read the various carriers' promotional information carefully. Does the carrier you're considering charge start-up or installation fees, or a flat monthly fee? If the latter, will you meet the carriers' minimum usage requirements, and are the services offered worth the monthly charge?

Other factors to consider include available volume discounts based on usage, and dedicated lines giving you exclusive access to a telecommunications network.

800 Numbers

Businesses that market products and services regionally or nationally have found the 800 number among their most effective marketing tools. Customers who might not otherwise pay for a call cross-country now pick up the phone without hesitation—and frequently wind up requesting further information or making hefty credit card purchases.

Though 800 numbers can pay for themselves thousands of times over, the installation fees, service charges, and usage fees can be expensive. Consider carefully whether the potential costs outweigh the benefits. An alternative is the localized 800 number, available for small, highly targeted geographic areas. Consult your phone company for further information.

Guidelines for Commercial Locations

Once volume expands to the point that operating your business from home is no longer practical, you may need to move to a commercial location.

Selecting the right location is vital to the success of your business. The first factors you must analyze when looking for a commercial location are: 1) the community you want to live and/or work in, based on family needs, finances, your preference for a particular area because of health reasons or the fact that you have an established reputation in a certain area; and 2) the locations available within that community.

These factors are interrelated. You may want to settle down in an area with a limited number of suitable business locations available. Or you may have run across a number of viable sites in several communities or areas, in which case an investigation of each must be conducted, covering each of the points listed below:

a) *The type of business you are planning to operate.* Retail, wholesale and service businesses have slightly different requirements as determined by the type of products or service being offered and the market potential in a specific area.

b) *The demographics of the area.* This includes the number of consumers who want or need your product or service and are willing and able to pay your price; the median income and employment opportunities; age ranges of the major population group; and the volume of retail trade and projected expansion data. This information is available from census reports and chamber of commerce business reports accumulated during your market research project.

c) *Competition.* You must determine how many other similar establishments are serving the market and how their businesses are going to decide if there is room for your new venture. The best way to do this is by compiling a list of businesses from the phone book that you feel will be in direct competition and, if applicable, visiting their locations at different times of day to observe the activity levels. You might also talk with employees, who should be willing to answer your questions if you approach them in a friendly way. Often, the same kind of research can be accomplished effectively on the telephone.

d) *Traffic patterns.* Is your proposed location close to freeways, major intersections and/or a central business district? Is there sufficient parking? Is the foot traffic past the location strong and steady enough to guarantee walk-in trade, if needed to generate sales and profits? The ease with which customers can get to your location is a major consideration in terms of success.

e) *Your image.* Decide on the image you want to project, such as top quality products, superior service, low prices, convenience, before you go scouting for locations.

f) *The product or service.* If, for example, you were planning to sell high priced, state-of-the-art European electronic equipment, it would be advisable to locate your business in a mall or on the main street of an economically comfortable community to ensure getting the response you need to survive. Generally, there are specific areas within a marketplace that cater to consumers in specific income levels and/or occupational groups, i.e., executives, blue collar workers, students, etc. Consider your product/service and the projected number of potential buyers within the community.

g) *The amount of rent required.* Locations having the highest potential of profit through consumer traffic (busy downtown areas, shopping malls, corner shops or stores with good frontage) are more expensive because competition keeps rents up to the maximum. The trade-off, however, is an increase in sales and, generally, a lower advertising budget because of the visibility factor.

As a new business owner, you may find that your allotted capital for rent is limited. Understanding and exploring the factors involved in selecting a location will help you find the best one for your money.

Retail Businesses

The guidelines indicated above are applicable for retail businesses. Poor location is one of the chief causes of failure among retail stores, but, on the other hand, the right location can be all it takes for even a mediocre business to thrive and grow.

Service Businesses

When clients are going to be visiting your place of business, the same principles of location selection apply as are indicated for retail. If clients will not be visiting, location selection can be based on rent, the amount of space needed and the convenience to you.

Wholesale or Manufacturing Businesses

Where you locate a wholesale business depends on your market. If dealing primarily with local retailers or customers, your location should be within easy driving distance of your clientele.

However, if most of your business is conducted through the mail or delivery services, you can base your selection on the best rent available and the convenience factor for you and your staff. When choosing a location for your wholesale business, warehousing needs are a vital consideration, as is projected expansion.

Before Signing a Lease

Unless you're planning to purchase the commercial location, rent your location from a family member or accept a temporary agreement in a location that is for sale, you will be required to sign a lease before moving in.

The most desirable agreement for you as a new business owner is a one-to-two year lease with a renewal option at a guaranteed rate for rent increases over a five to ten year period.

Rent for a commercial location is established either on a flat rate or a percentage basis. Under the flat rate, rent is generally based on the square footage of the shop and on the location or, in some cases, on potential volume. The percentage base involves a base amount of rent plus a pre-arranged percentage of monthly sales.

Your lease will also cover a number of other points, such as the liabilities and responsibilities of the landlord and of you, the tenant; i.e., who is to pay for specific repairs, renovations, tax increases and utilities, etc.

The lease may contain stipulations about the size of the exterior sign you can erect, hours of operation, insurance coverage and assignation of the lease to another party (a sublease).

Before signing a lease to set up your business, make sure that electrical lines are adequate enough to handle high volume usage, that you have restrooms for employees and/or clients, and convenient parking areas. Also check with the leasing agent to be certain you can make leasehold improvements (i.e., storage shelves, air conditioning, lighting) as the business warrants it.

It is recommended that you have an attorney review the lease carefully before you sign it to ensure that you understand all of the clauses and to serve as a negotiator, if necessary.

If setting up my business at home, I have:

- Checked with the city and county offices in my area regarding required licenses and permits and zoning regulations for home-as-office. _____
- Set aside a room or an area in my home that will be used exclusively for my business. _____
- Had a separate telephone installed and have purchased an answering machine or contracted with a message service. _____
- Set up a separate business bank account. _____
- Informed friends and family of my business routine and specific working hours to reduce interruptions and distractions. _____

If setting up in a commercial location, I have:

- Investigated rental rates for the area I am interested in. _____
- Checked traffic flow, parking and foot-traffic around my proposed location. _____
- Determined that my business is compatible with others in the area. _____
- Talked with my prospective landlord about improvements, maintenance and rent increases. _____
- Had my lawyer check the rental agreement and any local zoning regulations. _____
- Checked prices on storage units, work tables or shelves. _____
- Planned a layout that I feel will work well for the location and my storage, display and office needs. _____

6

SETTING UP YOUR BUSINESS AT HOME

There is a lot of appeal in operating your business from home.

Thousands of successful businesses have been started in a basement, a spare room or on the kitchen table. Henry Ford, for example, founded the Ford Motor Company in his garage and Jean Nidetch started Weight Watchers in her living room as a support group for friends who wanted to lose extra pounds. Both of these businesses, and many more like them, became successful multi-million-dollar corporations, despite humble beginnings.

The Small Business Administration estimates that there are close to 10 million home-based businesses in the United States today and, of these, more than 30% are owned and operated by women. These figures have been substantiated by an AT&T study, as well as by the U.S. Department of Labor.

Starting a home-based business has provided an opportunity for many people, who might otherwise never have the chance, to become entrepreneurs. Women, especially, have discovered that they can build a profitable, satisfying business at home while still being available for their families.

For others, a home-based business is the ticket out of the world of the urban commuter. In fact, a home-based business is the perfect way to try something new to see how it works while still working another job to pay the bills. Once the business has proven itself and is realizing a profit, you can leave the job to devote full time to your new venture.

Couples often find that investing time and energy in building a business together at home develops stronger relationships in addition to increasing joint income. For the retired and for those with minor physical disabilities, it is a path to staying involved, exploring self-sufficiency and guaranteeing a profitable future.

The Advantages of Establishing a Home-Based Business

- Ability to start your business immediately
- Minimal start-up capital needed
- No rent or excessive set-up charges for utilities required
- Comfortable working conditions
- Reduced wardrobe expenses
- No commuting
- Tax benefits
- Elimination of office politics
- Flexibility and independence
- Full utilization and recognition of skills
- Low risk for trial and error

Start-Ups Never Change

As with any new business whether located at home or in a commercial location, it is important to follow the basic guidelines for start-up, including: conducting a market survey, drawing up a business plan, setting goals, reviewing capital needs and projected income, developing an advertising campaign and establishing a professional image.

A medical claims business is, of course, tailored to the home, offering a number of advantages for the business owner who is just starting out.

Setting up your business at home automatically eliminates up to 75 percent of the start-up costs and responsibilities required for an office or storefront operation. You are, in your home, already making rent or mortgage payments and paying for your own telephone service, insurance and utilities.

In many instances, a commercial location will require $10,000 just to open the doors with basic leasehold improvements and/or equipment. In addition, valuable time and energy is saved in scouting for the location, having utilities installed and decorating the premises.

Getting Your Feet Wet

A home-based business gives you the opportunity to test the waters with a minimum of risk. This is especially beneficial to first time entrepreneurs, who may prefer to learn and grow with the business in the comfort of home without the pressures that operating out of a commercial location often brings.

As a hedge against inflation, the home-based business is a natural. In addition to low start-up, tax deductions (for use of your home as an office and your business expenses) provide relief from a seemingly endless outflow of cash on mortgage or rent payments. You must, however, be aware of the tax laws, which allow deductions only for that part of the home "used exclusively and regularly" for business and, as of last year, limited to a modified net income of the business.

After the business is running smoothly, you will find that the potential to earn money is greater because of reduced overhead. Your production will increase because you have more control over your schedule and fewer of the typical interruptions that arise in a commercial setting. Generally, home-based entrepreneurs claim that an added benefit is reduced stress, despite the fact that they are working long hours.

Of course, as with any business arrangement, there are also disadvantages to setting up your business in your home. By recognizing them, however, it is possible to address and minimize the problems before they come up.

Getting to Work

One of the biggest problems faced by home-based entrepreneurs is being able to establish a productive work schedule. There are different types of interruptions that come up in a home environment, including visits from friends and neighbors, household chores that need to be done, the temptation of television and the daily paper when there is work to be produced. There is also no one around to spur you on.

A helpful suggestion for getting down to work is to dress in the morning as if you were going out to a regular job. This alone will help you set your priorities for the day.

The best solution, however, is to establish regular working hours from the onset (although you do have the flexibility as a home-based business owner to arrange your schedule around the times you know you are the most productive). If friends want to visit, politely explain to them that you are operating a business which requires your full concentration and arrange a suitable time to get together according to your schedule.

It is also important, if you have family, that they are supportive and willing to arrange their lives as much as possible around your schedule. This can be dealt with through frequent family discussions about what you are doing and how the business operates.

Another difficult area is learning to separate business and pleasure. A home-based business often makes it very easy to work day and night on a project. Again, it is important to allot time for personal activities. The secret to remember is that the work will get done much more efficiently if you are relaxed and rested.

It's also a good idea to have the business set up in a separate room or area that can be shut off from your personal living space after working hours. This will more easily enable you to separate work from leisure time.

Home-based business owners often experience feelings of isolation from those in their industry.

One way to eliminate this is to join local groups, such as the chamber of commerce and networking groups, and to, at least, attend the meetings. Check to see how many members are entrepreneurs, which will give you a built-in support system. By making yourself available to serve on committees, you'll be able to reach into the community and publicize your business for the cost of your involvement.

The Disadvantages of Establishing a Home-Based Business

- Success is based 100% on your efforts
- Difficulty in establishing solid work habits
- Difficult to know how to set competitive rates
- Limited support system
- Isolation
- Limited work space
- Disruption of personal life
- Clients are uncomfortable coming to your home
- Zoning restrictions

Reviewing Local Laws

Before getting started, it is important to check that zoning ordinances in your area will allow you to use your home for business purposes. Since zoning ordinances vary from city to city and county to county, it is necessary to contact the Planning Department of your regional government offices or talk with your attorney to find out what is allowed. Regulations are based on the type of business, the area to be used within your home, noise control, tax regulations, business signs and other aspects. You may also need a special permit or license.

If you are expecting clients to visit your home for business, it is best to have a separate room set up as an office so that when they come to discuss a purchase, they won't feel as if they are intruding on a family. If, however, an office is out of the question, make sure you arrange meetings during times when the family is away from home to ensure that there will be no interruptions.

> *God gives every bird its food, but he does not throw it in the nest.*
>
> *J. G. Holland*

Another option is to go to the client's location when you must have meetings or to offer pick-up and delivery service, if applicable. Depending on the business, however, and the quality of your work, client discomfort shouldn't be a major problem, according to a number of home-based business owners we have interviewed.

As an example, the number of home-based typesetting services has increased dramatically over the past few years and we have never heard of any complaints or problems in this area. The bottom line, as far as the customer is concerned is still—and will always be—reliable service or high quality products and the knowledge that they are dealing with a professional.

The benefits of a home-based business to the beginning entrepreneur can mean the difference between working for someone else or turning a dream into reality.

The key element, as with any business, is motivation, a needed product or service, careful planning and the desire to succeed. But sometimes, just knowing that the expenses of establishing a business in a commercial location are alleviated by setting up a home-based enterprise is enough to push you forward to success, one small step after another.

7

START-UP BASICS: FIGURING COSTS

Having decided that you are ready and able to accept the challenge of starting your own business, it is necessary to take a look at your overall financial picture. Even if you have a healthy savings account, or feel you can start your business with a minimal capital investment, diagnosing your personal financial situation will help you determine on-going expenses.

The easiest way to estimate exactly how much money you will need to get your business started and to cover expenses, including personal living expenses, for the first six months is to prepare a *Cost of Living* or *Cash Flow Statement* and a *Projected Expense Chart*. Samples are provided on the following pages for your use.

Preparing the *Projected Expense Chart* will give you a fairly accurate picture of what it will cost to open the doors and indicate how much income you must generate to realize a profit. The other advantage of creating these charts early in the game is that when you do find that you want to explore funding options, you will already have two of the required documents prepared and will only need to update them.

Your first step is to ask yourself the following questions:

a) Do I generally pay my bills on time or wait until my creditors start sending me collection notices?

b) Have I regularly reconciled my bank statement so I know how much money I have in my checking account at any given time?

c) Is my philosophy "If I've got it, I spend it" or do I typically carefully plan how I am going to use my income?

d) Have I ever developed a personal budget so I know how much money is coming in, how much is going out and what I have left over?

These are important aspects of your financial personality that will be helpful to understand when running your business. As your business and subsequent involvement with financial matters grows, it will be vital that you have a handle on your philosophy about money. And there is no time like in the beginning, when your business concept is being formed, to start learning.

The Cash Flow Statement

Using the chart on Page 74, you can determine your personal living expenses for the past three to six months to help you gauge what you will need to survive during the early stages of your business.

The easiest way to complete the statement is to use your checkbook register, if you write checks for most purchases, and/or cash receipts and copies of money orders as research tools. If your expenses are relatively consistent from month to month, you should be able to get an overview by analyzing one month. A more accurate picture will emerge if you break down income and expense for three to six months to account for periodic payments, such as taxes, insurance and seasonal spending.

Using the samples provided, fill in the amounts in each category from your checkbook register or receipts. Use a separate sheet for every month that you are analyzing. For miscellaneous spending, a standard calculation is 5% of monthly income. Add up each month's expenses, total them all and then divide that figure by the number of months you are analyzing. This will give you an average month expense figure.

Follow the same procedure for income. You can then subtract your expenses from your income to see where you stand. If you have computed your figures accurately, you might run across a few surprises. It isn't unusual to discover that we spend more money than we realize, often on miscellaneous, unneeded purchases. You may be able to see some areas where you can cut back.

The main point, however, is that you now know a) how much or whether you can afford to invest your own money in your new business and b) what it costs you to live comfortably, which will help you set income goals for the business.

Cash Flow Statement
Month Of _____

Income		Expenses	
Wages	$_____	Rent or mortgage	$_____
Miscellaneous	_____	Auto loan	_____
		Gas & car repairs	_____
		Auto insurance	_____
TOTAL	$_____	Life insurance	_____
		Medical insurance	_____
		Homeowners insurance	_____
		Taxes	_____
Savings	$_____	Loan payments	_____
		Food: At home	_____
Credit Line	$_____	Food: Dining out	_____
		Telephone	_____
Home Equity	$_____	Utilities	_____
		Household repairs, etc.	_____
		Medical bills	_____
		Credit card payments	_____
		Interest expense	_____
		Clothing/dry cleaning	_____
		Travel	_____
		Miscellaneous	_____
		Savings	_____
		TOTAL	$_____

Start-Up Costs

Every business owner has specific standards about how they want to run their operation. One person may feel perfectly comfortable waiting until they are making a profit to order business cards. Another wouldn't dream of opening the doors without cards, brochures and letterhead already printed.

You will have your own ideas about what you need before opening your business. Then, you must find out what it will cost and, if at all possible, prepare the Start-Up Statement as outlined in this section.

It is also advisable to figure how much it will cost to run the business for three to six months, using the sample Projected Expense Forecast which follows. A six month projection should give you the opportunity to start getting an idea of your profits down the line.

Preparing the Start-Up Statement and Projected Expense Forecast involves conducting some research. For example, to estimate the cost of business cards or letterhead stationery, contact several printers or copy shops in your area and obtain quotes. Call the local newspaper for prices on different types of ads, including display and classified. An insurance agent will be able to give you an estimate on liability coverage. Check with the telephone company for information and rates on installing a phone line. You can also start to shop around to find the best prices on office supplies, equipment and materials needed to conduct business.

After completing your research, incorporate the information on the blank charts. Some of your figures, such as those for telephone expenses, will be "guesstimated." But the final figure will give you a good idea of start up and operational costs for the first six months.

Start-Up Costs

Furniture:	Purchase price	$_____	
	Down payment required		$_____
Fixtures:	Purchase price	$_____	
	Down payment required		$_____
Equipment:	Purchase price	$_____	
	Down payment required		$_____

Installation and deliver costs _____

Decorating & leasehold improvements _____

Deposits: Utilities and rent _____

Fees: Legal, accounting, consulting, etc. _____

Licenses & permits _____

Starting inventory _____

Supplies _____

Printing _____

Pre-opening advertising & promotion _____

Miscellaneous: _____

Total Start-Up Expense $_____

Less: Available Start-Up Capital (minus) $_____

Total Amount Needed $_____

Projected Expense Statement

Months:	1st	2nd	3rd	4th	5th	6th
Rent						
Utilities						
Telephone						
Insurance						
Professional Services						
Taxes & Licenses						
Advertising						
Office Supplies						
Office Equipment						
Inventory						
Business auto expense						
Travel expense						
Entertainment						
Dues & subscriptions						
Salaries						
Owner's draw						
Loan payments						
Interest payments						
Miscellaneous						
TOTALS						

Have this sample chart enlarged at your local copy shop if planning to use it as part of your Business Plan. Enlarging it will cost you a few cents, but can save you many dollars in the long run, because of the increased awareness of your financial picture.

Utilizing the same theory, you can develop a Projected Income Statement, drawing from industry figures available through your trade association or other research sources.

This would include all income realized from cash sales, collection on outstanding invoices, credit card sales and miscellaneous income. By subtracting your total expenses from total income, you will get a clear picture of projected profit or loss.

All of these statements will be requested by loan officers, venture capitalists and the Small Business Administration (SBA) if and when you apply for a loan. They require this kind of paperwork to ensure that you have basic business knowledge and a commendable track record, and are serious about your venture. You will also be required to fill out a personal financial statement, available through the lending institution, especially if you are the sole owner or a general partner in the business.

8

BASIC REQUIREMENTS: EQUIPMENT & SUPPLIES

As we've mentioned throughout this business guide, having the right equipment will make or break your new business.

The Computer Is King

For both medical claims and medical transcription, the computer will be the center of your entire operation. It will perform all manner of word processing, billing, formatting and calculations. Choosing the right one, however, may be a little tricky.

Currently, the majority of medical claims and transcription is performed on IBM/PC-compatible (or clone) computers, with a smaller percentage of the population using the Macintosh. This isn't saying that one is better than the other; it's due to the fact that there are more software programs available on the clones because they've been around longer. This fact should help you decide which one is right for you.

Look at the software that is currently available for the business that you're getting into. Medical transcription uses word processing programs to get the job done. Word processors are almost identical on both the IBM/PC-compatible and Macintosh platforms. Word and WordPerfect are the two industry leaders and their abilities are just about equal. So either computer should work just fine.

Medical claims requires more specific software, like MediSoft's Patient Accounting or Absolute Software's Medical ProClaim!, which are available only on the IBM/PC.

Specific Software

Medical transcription is primarily done in either Microsoft Word or WordPerfect. These programs are readily available through any software retail or mail order outlet. The average price for Word or WordPerfect runs around $300.

A word processor alone is only half the arsenal you need to be truly productive as a medical transcriptionist. Having an electronic dictionary (standard, medical, drug and specialty) will speed up your research time immensely. You will be able to look up a word and definition faster than with a normal reference book. Stedman's *Electronic Medical Dictionary* ($129), Spellex's *Medical and Pharmaceutical Dictionaries* ($100), and Dorland's *Electronic Medical Speller* ($89) are all industry standards.

Another add on that is essential for your computer is a macro program like Productivity Software's *PRD+* ($95) or Sylvan's *Fast Forward* ($80). These macro programs shorten your typing time by "learning" what you are typing and automatically filling in the words when you start the first few letters. For example, start typing "ex" and "examination" pops up. Or type abbreviations such as "heent" and "head, eyes, ears, nose & throat" is entered. (You can see how that would save you quite a bit of time.)

There are a few different medical claims billing software packages available. These tend to cost more than the transcription programs because of the complex functions they perform—processing, storing, printing, sending, editing and archiving. They can handle all the tasks you will need to perform for your claims business—saving you a lot of work, money and time. MediSoft Advanced Patient Accounting ($499) and Absolute Medical ProClaim! ($595) are two programs that are widely used.

One add-on program that is worth investing in is a CPT & ICD-9 Code database, since each claim needs to have a procedure or diagnosis code listed with a description. Having all these codes (over 30,000) instantly accessible is an incredible time saver. MediSoft offers their Codes on Disk ($99 per medical specialty).

References

Reference books will still be necessary even if you have specific medical and grammatical software. A good, large medical dictionary like Dorland's *Illustrated Medical Dictionary* ($40), a drug dictionary like Saunders' *Pharmaceutical Word Book* ($30), a medical word speller by specialties (various, $10 to $40), a laboratory book like the *Surgical Word Book* ($30), and any specialty books that would apply to the area in which you work, will also speed up the job.

Grammar guides and style books like the *AAMT Book of Style for Medical Transcription* ($50), Strunk and White's *The Elements of Style* ($9), and *The Elements of Grammar* ($9) are all very valuable resources.

Dictation Equipment

Medical transcription needs another vital component for day-to-day operations—the dictation machine. You will be using this item almost as much as your computer, so investing in a durable and easy-to-use model is worthwhile.

The features to look for in a dictation machine include a footswitch (to start and stop the machine), headset (for close listening) and speed controls (to speed up the dictation for proofreading).

The Modem

If you are planning on sending medical claims, or even finished transcription for that matter, electronically to the clearing house or provider, the only way to do this is with a modem (modulator-demodulator). A modem hooks up to your computer with a standard cable on one end, and to the phone line on the other. It translates your computer information into a form that will travel over the telephone line and to its destination instantly. (For more information on modems, see page 85).

Home Learning Products

If you are brand new to this industry, you will need additional help sorting out all the information that is bombarding you now. You may wish to enroll in a home learning course or simply study on your own. Either way focusing on your learning will keep you headed in the right direction.

For the beginning transcriptionist, The Independent Medical Transcriptionist, from Rayve Productions 800-852-4890 ($34.95) is a good step-by-step reference for running your operations and getting familiar with the specific terms and procedures.

Or if you want the structure of a home study course, Health Professions Institute, At-Home Professions and California College for Health Sciences all offer programs that train you to be a qualified medical transcriptionist (see Resources section for addresses and phone numbers).

For medical claims, MediSoft and AAMA offer complete start-up packages including Billing Service Training videos, manuals and marketing kits. Their programs will show you the proper procedures and work hints to expand your knowledge and experience, along with providing you all the reference materials, audio tapes and forms that will become valuable assets for your business.

Computer System

One of your basic needs will be a good word processor, enabling you to easily perform a wide variety of tasks from marketing to billing.

Computer prices are dropping rapidly, and you can currently buy a perfectly good used system for under $500; check the classifieds of local publications. If you wish to have the latest and greatest, expect to pay $1,500 to $3,000 for it. If you have the time to shop around, you can purchase a good computer system for between $700 and $1,500. Also, look for new-merchandise bargains at grand openings of computer stores, year-end closeouts, etc.

Frequently, the computer you purchase will come equipped with word processing and other proprietary software packages, so shop around for the best deal.

Software

There are a number of software packages well-suited to run a medical claims operation. However, you don't necessarily need an industry-specific software package, as long as the business software package you choose has the following: accounting; the ability to link to other software systems; word processing; report generation; and a graphics capability.

When choosing a software package, begin by analyzing all the essential elements: everything from data processing to accounting. Then contact computer stores and software manufacturers for information, brochures, etc. Make sure the software is compatible with your hardware if you already own a computer; otherwise, tailor the hardware to the best software package(s).

Arrange for a software demonstration, and bring along your list of requirements. If you're not computer-literate, bring along someone who is, and during the demonstration be sure to use the equipment yourself, making sure it's user-friendly.

Most important, compare each software system with your needs, not the features of other systems. You ultimately are the one who has to use the program and be satisfied with it. If it costs hundreds of dollars and has a lot of bells and whistles you'll never need or use, keep looking. Shop carefully and base your choice on your own business projections and the market you'll be serving. One alternative is to buy an integrated package— one combining several applications (word processing, accounting, database management, and so on).

> *One alternative is to buy an integrated package combining several applications, from accounting to word processing and database management.*

The leading packages in all software categories are too numerous to outline here. What follows is a glance at the proven winners and most commonly used programs (most are available both for IBM-compatibles and Macintosh):

spreadsheet/accounting (Lotus 1-2-3, Excel); database management (Paradox, dBASE, Quattro Pro); word processing (WordPerfect, Microsoft Word); graphics (CorelDraw!, QuickDraw); and integrated software (Microsoft Works is generally considered one of the best available).

Printers

Printers are broken down into three categories: laser (essential for high-quality graphic and desktop publishing applications), dot-matrix (still the biggest seller, and acceptable for a range of applications from correspondence to billing), and ink-jet (used for graphic and business applications).

Laser. Hewlett-Packard dominates much of the laser market with its LaserJet series. Ask your computer dealer for the lowest-cost LaserJet (at this writing Hewlett-Packard makes a good low-cost alternative perfect for the home office). Also consider low-cost offerings from Okidata.

Dot-matrix. Popular choices here include printers from Epson, Panasonic, Okidata, and Microline. If you don't have a need for high-quality graphic output, and plan to use your computer for correspondence and accounts payable/receivable, dot-matrix printers are the low-cost way to go.

Ink jet. Again, the leader in this category is Hewlett-Packard with a popular DeskJet series that comes in both black-and-white and color models.

Modems

Modems transmit and receive computer data over telephone lines, connecting the home or office-based business with the outside world, from a print shop down the street to a client in Europe.

Modems usually are categorized by their transmission (or baud) rate, measured in bits (or characters) per second. Baud rates are typically 300, 1200, and 2400, but more commonly are upwards of 9600. Modems 1200 baud and higher are recommended for long documents. The higher the baud rate, the faster the transmission time and thus the lower your phone bill, since transmission time is billed in the same manner as a phone call. A recent addition to the modem family is the fax modem, turning your phone into an all-purpose retrieval/transmission center.

Notebooks

These lightweight, battery-powered laptops can be used as stand alone systems or as add-ons to your home computer, in both cases providing system access at remote locations—from the back seat of a limo or a 747 at 30,000 feet. They're more costly than their more conventional counterparts (upwards of $2,500), but can be worth the expense if you frequently need computer access at a variety of locations.

> *Battery-operated laptop computers provide system access from the backseat of a limo or a 747 at 30,000 feet*

CD-ROMs

The storage medium of the future has not only arrived, it's standard equipment on a number of computer systems, enabling users to store 150,000 pages of text per disc and take a massive load off their hard drives. CD-ROMs store everything from downloaded fonts to 60-million-word dictionaries, and represent the 21st century's ultimate interactive resource. They'll eventually replace conventional newspapers and libraries, becoming the central link in home information systems.

Fax Machines

Fax machines have become standard equipment in commercial offices and increasingly in the home office, allowing local or worldwide transmission of information in a matter of seconds.

Fax machines come in a variety of sizes, from affordable compact models (recommended for the small business) to larger floor-standing units. Some models are also combination answering machines and flatbed copiers. Some of the higher-end systems use laser printer technology well suited to graphics-oriented data.

Some of the smaller units are now available new for about $275 (shop carefully) and can be bought on the used market for considerably less. Leading manufacturers include Canon, Xerox, and Sharp.

Furniture and Supplies

You will need basic office furniture when expanding your business. Whenever possible buy used furniture. A desk for general marketing and billing is of course essential. But if you plan on computerizing, you'll also need a computer desk with room for a printer and modem. You'll also need shelving for computer disks, books, and other miscellaneous items.

Consider the benefits of a good calculator with tape for billing and record-keeping and shelves for storing a library of reference books and other relevant publications. You'll also need such standard supplies as card files, file cabinets, and staplers. In addition, you'll need letterhead stationery, business cards, printed envelopes, and brochures that explain your service.

All are available at local stationers and office supply stores. For record-keeping, you'll need index cards, large manila envelopes, files, and invoice forms. Even with a computer storing a lot of your data, these items are still necessary.

Check for wholesale distributors in your area or ask other business people for good suppliers. Get estimates from two or three suppliers before making a final decision. Business supplies can be obtained from mail order companies as well.

Buy or Lease? Making the Choice

You can buy new or used equipment from dealers and independent sellers. Or, if you don't mind rummaging through other people's lives, you can find incredible bargains on supplies and equipment at garage sales, swap meets, thrift shops run by charitable organizations or auctions. Often, it is well worth the time involved because the savings can be tremendous.

Before investing money, do your homework. Talk with other business owners to find out which brand of equipment they use and why they prefer it over other choices on the market. This will help you make the best decision based on your needs and budget.

Also, talk with independent dealers who carry a broad line of similar types of equipment. They can give you insights on maintenance, longevity, service contracts and prices.

They will also be able to tell you when to expect a drop in price for the item you are interested in, although you can count on seeing sales on major equipment such as computers and other big-ticket items at store openings and during special sales.

Cash or Credit?

Unless you are planning to pay cash for an equipment purchase, you will either make a down payment and set up a payment schedule with the dealer or take out a loan with the bank. With interest rates for bank loans currently running at about 9-12%, you might be able to find a dealer who is willing to handle the financing at a lower rate.

Although this method is a less effective way of establishing creditworthiness, it will serve to get the business going. Another advantage is that if you should find yourself in a tight cash flow situation at any time, a private dealer/lender with whom you have a personal relationship is much more likely to be flexible . . . without charging you a penalty for late payment.

Buying Used Equipment

When buying used equipment from a dealer, the chances of it being in working condition are generally pretty good. Dealers have a reputation to uphold and will stand behind their merchandise, especially if they are firmly established in the community. There are, however, several ways you can scout around to ensure that the one you decide to work with is reputable:

• Find a store with membership in the local chamber of commerce. Although this is not an ironclad guarantee, it does indicate the store ownership's interest in following business standards established within the community.

• If the dealer also sells new equipment, it is highly likely that much of the used equipment has been traded in by people who are upgrading. You may be able to get an excellent bargain on an item which has been well maintained by the former owner.

• If there is a service department on the premises, you can be assured that used equipment has been reconditioned before being put on sale. It also increases your chances of getting fast, inexpensive and reliable service if needed at a later date.

• Used equipment dealers realize that it is not always easy to find a buyer and should be willing to work with you. Shopping around will give you an idea of average prices and will give you the information you need to negotiate. If the dealer won't work with you, keep looking.

• What are the terms of the warranty? Even used equipment should be covered for a short time for parts and labor, especially if it has been overhauled or reconditioned.

• Is the dealer willing to agree to offer a trade-in allowance on the item you are buying when you decide to upgrade? Of course, there will be stipulations based on wear and tear and time; however, he or she should be willing to consider it.

Buyer Beware

There are other ways to find and buy used equipment, but it falls into the realm of "Buyer Beware." If you choose to deal with private parties through the classified ads or with auctioneers selling off the inventory of a bankrupt business, you must be willing to take a chance. Although the prices will be easy on your budget, the cost of repairing a malfunctioning machine could result in a long-term drain on your profits.

This is not to say that there aren't bargains out there. In many cases, you will stumble across an incredible deal on a "like-new" computer, as an example. The secret is to know what you are looking for and to have a good idea of how it

> *The greatest inspiration is a challenge to attempt the impossible*
>
> *A. Michelson*

should work. Do your research by visiting with reliable used equipment dealers before you start looking.

When talking with a private party, ask them how long they have owned the equipment, why they are selling it and if they have kept any repair bills that you can see. Trust your intuition in this kind of situation; if the person seems truly interested in providing you with as much information as possible, chances are the equipment is everything they say it is or isn't. If they tell you it needs a new part, for example, find out what the replacement part costs and ask if they would deduct it from the selling price.

When you go to see the equipment, make sure it runs. Test it out if possible, measure it to make sure it will fit into the space you have available and decide whether you can move it yourself or will have to arrange transportation. Before buying it, try to find out whether there is a servicing outlet nearby or if you must send away for parts, which can be time-consuming and costly, especially when it comes to older models.

Referral Discounts

Here's a way to boost your income that will make your clients happy to promote the business.

Offer clients who provide you with the name of a potential listing (or who have someone call you) a discount on billing. If it results in a job, give a ten percent discount to the referring party.

Occasionally you will run across an individual who is making payments on a piece of equipment still under warranty. This can be a great deal for you since they will probably accept a small amount of cash and let you take over the payments. Be sure to transfer ownership in writing to prevent complications if you need service under the warranty.

Auctions

Auctions are an excellent way to get good bargains. Watch the business and classified sections of the newspaper for ads about upcoming auctions. The ad will include dates, the reason for the auction (liquidation or bankruptcy), location, time and a partial list of items. In most cases, there will be a preview, enabling potential buyers to view the merchandise before the bidding begins.

By all means, take advantage of the preview to inspect and select equipment you want to bid on. A fee will be required for a bidder registration number, which is held up when you make a bid so the auctioneer's spotters know who has purchased a particular item.

The two rules to remember at auctions are: a) cash or a personal check for the full purchase amount must be paid on the day of the auction and b) don't move your hands or make significant gestures during bidding or you might find that you have purchased something you didn't want.

Leasing Equipment

Leasing is defined as a long-term agreement between two parties for the use of a specific item. The person who leases is known as the lessee, while the owner of the item is referred to as the lessor. Despite the fact that you do not own the equipment when you lease and so can not take advantage of depreciation on it for tax purposes, there are still many benefits for the beginning business owners.

Leasing lets you try out a piece of equipment for a given period of time to determine if it is the best product for your needs. Although you are locked into the terms of the lease, most lessors are flexible.

Know What You Need

Of course, the way to prevent this in the first place is to be absolutely clear about what you expect the equipment to do for you. The service representative from the leasing company is well-versed in tailoring equipment to customer, so do not hesitate to ask questions about capabilities.

Most lessors offer good maintenance contracts as they want to protect their equipment. Check to see what parts and/or labor are covered before signing the lease. The lessor should also be willing to provide technical advice at no charge, may be willing to offer installation and set-up of the equipment and also provide training, if required.

Payments can be arranged to fit your budgetary needs on a monthly, semi-annual or annual basis. This gives you the freedom to schedule payments for peak cash-flow periods. You can also negotiate the rates and length of time of the lease to keep monthly operating expenses at a minimum.

Conditional Sales Agreement

Under the provisions of a conditional sales agreement, you become the owner of the leased goods from the agreement date. At the end of the lease period, you are required to purchase the item for a pre-established price. This is often referred to as a balloon payment and should be agreed upon by you and the lessor prior to your signing the lease.

The conditional sales agreement, unlike most other leasing contracts, gives you the tax advantage of claiming depreciation on equipment. Depreciation refers to the decrease in the value of an asset because of wear and tear over a period of time.

You are entitled to deduct depreciation, based on value when new, the estimated life of the item and the value at the end of that estimated life, from your income tax. It is best to work with your accountant on determining depreciation of fixed assets.

There is seldom a down payment, other than the first month's lease amount, required on a leased item, since leasing is generally 100 percent financed for the terms of the agreement. This frees your start-up or working capital for other uses.

True Lease Agreements

You can write off lease payments on your income tax, but only if you have a true lease contract. Under a true lease, the lessor owns the equipment at all times during the contract period. If you decided, at the end of the lease, that you wanted to buy the equipment, you would have to pay whatever purchase price was decided by the lessor.

Financial Lease

The financial lease covers a period that does not extend beyond the estimated life of the equipment. Payments must be made as stipulated on the date due and through to the end of the lease. It usually puts the responsibility and cost of maintenance on the lessee.

Operating Lease

The operating lease generally requires the lessor to handle maintenance of the equipment. It offers the option of cancelling the lease, but only if a cancellation clause has been included at the negotiating stage.

The most important aspects of leasing are the terms outlined in the formal lease. Have the lessor draw up a proposal for you, based on everything you have discussed in an initial meeting. If you have any trouble understanding the terms of the proposal, have your attorney review it with you. In fact, it is a definite advantage to have the final lease agreement checked by your attorney or accountant before you sign it.

What Your Lease Agreement Should Include

- The length of the contract in months or years.
- The rate you are to be charged, which is usually a percentage of the total purchase price computed on a monthly rate.
- Your payment schedule.
- Purchase option, if applicable, at the end of the lease.
- Renewal option, if applicable, which allows you to carry the lease over for an additional period of time.
- Cancellation agreement in the event you want or need to cancel the lease.
- Maintenance stipulations (who pays for parts & labor).
- Substitution options if updated equipment is introduced and you want to take advantage of improvements.
- Any provisions particular to the lease, including tax allowances for depreciation, insurance liability in case of loss or damage and your responsibilities in reporting a move or other major change.

Whether you decide to borrow, buy new equipment, find good used equipment or lease, be sure to get exactly what you need to keep costs at a minimum. This is especially important during the early stages of your business when cash is bound to be tight. You can always upgrade or add to your equipment inventory as profits increase.

9

SELECTING PROFESSIONALS

From the start-up stage and as your business continues to grow and prosper, you will need the assistance of several professionals, including a lawyer, an accountant and an insurance agent.

The best way to find a professional is, according to the majority of business owners, through personal recommendations from other entrepreneurs, especially those in similar businesses as yours, and from friends or relatives. The most important factor is that the person doing the recommending understands exactly what you will need from the professional you will be hiring.

For example, your cousin's divorce lawyer is probably not as well suited to helping you draw up a partnership agreement as the attorney a friend used to help them incorporate their business.

Before making a decision, talk to several recommended professionals until you find someone who can best satisfy your needs for the business as outlined below and who has a fee structure you can afford. Equally important is that it is someone whom you feel comfortable with, especially during those times when you are forced by external forces to call five times a week to resolve a problem or complete a specific task. In many cases, because attorneys and accountants often work on a particular business matter in conjunction with one another, the attorney you select may be able to suggest an accountant who can properly service your business, or vice versa.

If you are planning to hire an attorney or an accountant, you should start "interviewing" likely candidates eight to nine months prior to the date you plan to start the business. This will give you time to find a suitable match and give them time to take care of all pre-startup functions, such as establishing your business form and helping you with your business plan.

What to Expect from Professional Services

Legal

You need an attorney with broad-based expertise in business who can help you with such matters as raising capital, legal and tax ramifications and the benefits of various business forms including sole proprietorship, partnership or corporation. Also important are name clearance (to ensure that you are not using a name already designated by another company), legal tips on operating in your desired location, and the ability to file all necessary legal papers and documents needed for financing and establishing your business.

He or she will review contracts and lease agreements, and can provide support with collection problems. The lawyer you select should also be willing and able to represent you in the event of any claims that are brought against you or lawsuits you initiate.

Fees

Depending on your lawyer's expertise, reputation and where he/she is located (metropolitan area versus small town, for example), fees will differ dramatically. In a smaller community, lawyers often charge a set rate for the job being done while "city" lawyers typically charge by the hour with fees ranging anywhere from $65 to $250 per hour.

This does not include the extraneous expenses involved, such as the $300 to $1,000 cost of incorporating, depending on the state you operate in. Fees also do not include supplemental costs, such as travel and telephone, incurred by the attorney in the handling of your case.

A good way to get an idea of what to expect in the way of fees in your area is to check with your local chamber of commerce or the state bar association, generally located in the capital city. The bar association may also be able to provide you with information about a particular attorney's reputation and expertise.

When talking with potential attorneys—and when you have found one who is compatible to your needs—always be sure to ask for an outline of expenses and also find out if they are willing to notify you when the fees for a particular job will be exceeded.

Accounting

The accountant you select should, early on, be able to work with you on putting together your business plan, including your projected profit and loss statements, for financing.

Down the line as your business is being established, the accountant will help you set up your books and, once in operation, should handle your tax returns, prepare financial statements and offer financial advice regarding tax matters, cash flow, investments to maximize the use of profits and the tax regulations regarding employees, when you are ready to hire.

Fees

As with attorneys, there is a professional association in your state capital which certifies and maintains records on the reputation and fee structures of accountants. The basis for fee structuring does vary slightly, however, with accountants. Some charge by the hour, others by the day and still others work on a set monthly retainer, based on the estimated amount of time they will be required to spend on your work. Hourly fees, however, average between $25 and $100 depending on expertise and location.

Insurance

Before setting out on your search for an insurance agent, it is advisable to have already established your business form and learned exactly what insurance the law in your area requires you to carry (fire, liability, etc.) And if you will be hiring employees, find out what kind of program you want to offer, as well as what you will need for your own medical and life insurance.

The insurance agent you choose should be familiar with the needs of businesses and business owners, not just the standard life and disability policies. Your insurance needs will change as your business grows and expands (i.e., employee health, workman's compensation, etc.). At that point, you may want to consider key person coverage to insure that a small company can survive if a major partner or employee dies.

There are also a number of pension programs and stock-option programs available in the event you want to offer employees the incentive to increase their participation in the company in exchange for partial "ownership" down the line.

Fees

The fees for your agent's expertise are paid from your premiums, and there should definitely not be any extra charge to you for advice or administration of your insurance policies and programs.

10

TAXES, LICENSES AND PERMITS

$\mathbf{A}$s a business owner, you are responsible for the timely report filing and payment of federal, state and local taxes. Whether you have an accountant prepare your returns, or do it yourself, the task will be made much easier if you establish a systematic record-keeping system as reviewed in Chapter 14 and keep your records accurate and up-to-date.

This includes maintaining all written documents pertaining to the financial aspect of your business; invoices, bank statements, receipts of any and all business expenses and deposit slips.

One of the easiest ways to keep control of the "paper dragon" is to set up a 9 x 12 inch manila envelope or a file folder for each of the following categories: paid bills—both personal and business; sales receipts of every product you've sold or service job performed; Inventory records based on on-going inventory control and quarterly audits; copies of invoices or billing statements that are paid with a separate file for those still due you; receipts for miscellaneous cash purchases; auto and entertainment receipts from travel and promotional activities.

All of these documents must be kept for at least five years to substantiate deductions claimed on your income tax returns in the event of an I.R.S. audit. Make up new file folders or envelopes at the beginning of each year and store the old ones in a safe place.

It is not only a time-consuming task that can take you away from the important job of running your business, but preparing income tax returns, especially for the federal government, has become almost an art form. Tax law is a constantly changing, complicated fact of life. It is strongly recommended that you have an accountant lined up to prepare your taxes and keep you informed of any pertinent changes during the year.

Business Deductions

The deductions that you will most likely qualify for as a business owner include expenses incurred for the operating of business, such as telephone, postage, advertising, bank service charges, travel and expense of conventions, interest, dues to professional organizations and subscriptions to magazines pertaining to your business, among others.

If you have established your business at home, you will be able to deduct that portion of the house used exclusively for business, as well as a percentage of your costs for telephone service and utilities.

Again, because of the complexity and obscurity of many of the deductions, it is best to have a professional do your taxes to ensure you get the full benefits you are entitled to.

The list on the following page provides an overview of the tax returns which may be applicable to your business situation. It is meant only to inform you. Filing requirements will be determined by the type of business, the legal structure (sole proprietorship, partnership or corporation), income from the business, your location, state and local laws and whether or not you have employees.

For example, as the sole proprietor of your business you would probably only be required to file personal federal and state returns based on profit or loss with the appropriate schedules for business expenses, pay sales, self-employment and estimated taxes, local business license fees and sales tax.

Federal Tax Returns

Form 1040: Income tax for Sole Proprietors,
    Partners or S Corporation shareholders.
Schedule C: Profit (or Loss) from Business or Profession.
Form 1065: Partnership income tax return.
Schedule K-1: Partner's share of Income, Credits,
    Deductions, etc.
Form 1120: Corporation tax return with applicable
    support schedules.
Form 2553: S Corporation Filing
Form 1120-S: S Corporation Tax Return
Form 1040ES: Quarterly Estimated Tax for
    Sole Owner or Partner.
Form 1120W: Quarterly Estimated Tax for Corporation.
Form 940: Federal Unemployment (Social Security)
    Tax for Sole Owner, Partner, Corporations.
Schedule SE: Annual return of self-employment tax
    for Sole Proprietor or Partner.

State Income Tax

Each state has corresponding filing requirements; however, form and schedule numbers vary. Contact your State Franchise Tax Board or your accountant for details.

Local Taxes

Taxes will vary from city to city and county to county; however, you may be required to pay city income tax, local sales tax as well as real or personal property taxes. Check with your local government offices for specifics.

Licenses and Permits

To operate your business, you will need permits and licenses based on the requirements in your area and the type of business you are running. You will probably, however, be required to obtain the following documents no matter where you live.

Local Business License

Basically this is simply a fee paid to the city or county in which you are located which allows you to operate your business in that area. Some cities will also require you to pay a percentage of your gross sales every year.

Fictitious Name Statement

This is a registration for protection of your business name. Filing for the fictitious name statement will also involve a city or county-wide search to make sure you are not duplicating an existing name. See details in "Naming Your Business" in chapter 11.

Seller's Permit or Resale Certificate

Required only if you are going to be charging sales tax. Services are often exempt.

Health Permit

Required only if you are preparing or distributing food in any manner. Involves an initial inspection and sporadic follow-up inspections by health department officials.

Taxpayer Identification Number

Available from the I.R.S. by filing Form SS-4, in the case of partnerships, S corporations or corporations. Sole proprietors are required to have a taxpayer identification number if they pay wages to one or more employee or file pension or excise tax forms.

Your local governmental offices or your attorney will be able to give you information on the specific licenses and permits, and required fees for each as required in your case.

Legal Structure

As a self-employed business owner, you are required to decide on a legal form of business for tax reporting purposes. There are four basic classifications, as outlined below. If, after reviewing them, you are still unsure of which way to go, it would be advisable to talk with a lawyer about the advantages and disadvantages of each structure for your particular business.

Sole Proprietorship

This is the easiest to establish and the preferred structure for many small business owners. A proprietorship is relatively free from government regulation, as the business has no existence apart from the owner. Profits from the operation of business are treated as personal income for purposes of taxation and your proprietary interest ends when you die or dissolve the business.

The major drawback of a proprietorship is that you are personally liable for any and all claims against the business and undertake the risks of the business to the extent of all assets, whether they are used in the business or personally owned. As a sole proprietor, you will be required to file self-employment tax returns and ordinarily would have to make estimated tax payments on a quarterly basis.

General Partnership

This is also easy to set up and administer. Since responsibilities and capitalization are usually shared by two or more partners, taxation is based on each partner's share of business income and determined by their individual tax rates. Again, claims against the business can be filed against personal assets and financial liability is shared equally by all partners.

Limited Partnership

This structure can be established when one or more people are willing to invest cash or tangible property in the business with active participation in the daily operations. However, there must be at least one general partner who carries unlimited financial liability and usually maintains a full-time managerial position within the company.

The limited partner(s) are liable only for business debts up to the amount of their investment. Although a partnership is not a taxable entity, it must figure its profit or loss and file an annual tax return, which also becomes part of the partners' personal returns.

Corporation

In this structure, stock or shares in the business are sold to investors or stockholders, who then control the company. The advantage is that corporate stockholders are removed from any liability against personal assets. The most anyone can lose in the event of bankruptcy or a liable claim is their stock.

The privilege of reduced liability, however, creates paperwork (articles of incorporation and annual reports for the state tax commission and federal regulators); expenses (filing and licensing fees) and double taxation (the corporation is taxed on profits, while stockholders and elected officers are taxed individually on wages and/or dividend income).

Subchapter S Corporation

This structure has proved to be a real boon for small business owners who want the benefit of corporate protection from personal liability without double taxation. In a Subchapter S corporation, a maximum of 35 stockholders (who can be family members) report their share of corporate income on individual tax returns.

The corporation itself is generally exempt from federal income tax; however, it may be required to pay a tax on excess net passive investment income, capital gains or built-in gains. To structure your company as a Subchapter S corporation, all of the shareholders must consent to the choice.

All businesses, regardless of size, are required to maintain detailed records and file the necessary tax returns. In a corporation, regular meetings must be held. The stockholders elect a board of directors, who establish and monitor corporate policy. The board selects corporate officers to conduct the operations of the business.

Sole proprietorships are the most convenient and least complicated form of business organizations for new business owners, especially in the early stages. As your business grows, you will want to explore the options as a way of protecting your personal assets and increasing the potential for expansion capital.

11

NAMING YOUR BUSINESS

As a pet owner, it is unlikely that you would give your German Shepherd a name like Fifi. It wouldn't suit the dog's image, nor would it be appropriate. The same principle applies to choosing a name for your business.

The name you select for your business can be a tremendous asset when it defines the kind of image you want to project. You want the name to attract and appeal to potential customers, to be easily remembered over that of the competition's, and be appropriate to the type of business you are starting.

Today's consumers are constantly bombarded with advertising as they go about their daily routines. Getting their attention, and holding it long enough for them to make an association between your business name and what you are offering, is imperative.

A memorable moniker can mean the difference between continued growth or a mediocre response from an audience victimized by information overload. (It is, of course, important to remember that your ultimate success depends on well designed advertising, careful planning, and quality products and/or service).

Naming your Medical Claims & Transcription Business

Take some time to think about this, because your company name needs to fulfill several functions beyond identifying you. The name you choose can affect a customer's perceptions of your legitimacy.

It may serve you best to just use your own name, e.g., Mary's Medical Claims & Transcription.

Depending on where you live, there may be a number of other Medical Claims & Transcription businesses with names that are similar to the one you want. Set yourself apart from the flock. Choose a name that is catchy and descriptive, and then come up with a logo that says something about who you are.

Brainstorming

Start by making a list of all the positive aspects of your business that you can think of, and call on friends and relatives to provide as many as they can come up with. Write down all the possibilities, no matter how funny or unusual they seem. A handy tool for business naming is the thesaurus, which will give you a vast number of options for commonplace names. Consider everything that springs forth from your imagination.

When you have created a list of likely candidates, get together with a group of supportive friends and family members and have a brainstorming session to either pick one of the choices you have come up with or to develop something from the ideas listed. Chances are that within a few hours, you will have a name for your business.

Catchy names are fun to design. However, make sure it isn't so offbeat, cute, or trendy as to risk slipping into obscurity as time passes.

The Fictitious Name Statement

You are required to file a fictitious name statement with the county clerk's office where you will be basing the business. While there, you should be able to do a countywide name check on the spot to see if there are any other businesses in the region using the name you have selected. The filing fee depends on where you live, and must be done within thirty days after you officially open your business.

It will also be necessary to publish the fictitious name in a local newspaper; the cost depends on the circulation of the paper. The county clerk's office will advise you about specific requirements in your area.

If you are starting a business that will be operating in a broader market, statewide or nationally, it is important to have your attorney do a name clearance investigation, which can take from three days to three weeks.

Your Visual Image

After you have selected a name that reflects your business image, the next step is translating it into a visual symbol or logo (logo type) to serve as a signature piece for your business. Often this involves creating a visual interpretation of your company name, but in other cases a graphic symbol or trademark is designed to serve as identification.

Some established corporate trademarks are so familiar that you can immediately identify the company even without seeing or hearing its name.

A good example of this includes the logo of the dog with his head cocked to one side. The accompanying copy reads "His Master's Voice," and it's a good bet that you recognize this as the logo for RCA. Another effective logo is the avant-garde apple that identifies Apple computer products.

If you do not have the graphic skills necessary to design a logo with impact, get in touch with your nearest art association (listed in the phone book or available through local art supply shops or galleries) or call a nearby college or university. Ask the head of the art department if your design can be given as a class assignment or if he or she could recommend a student to do the job for a small fee. It will give students practical application, and the design can be used later in their portfolios. You can offer cash or a prize for the best design. The students will undoubtedly meet the challenge with enthusiasm and give you a number of good samples and ideas from which to choose.

Selecting a Typeface

Save sample logos and advertisements that use a typeface you like. Type is an extremely important element of logo design and can also pinpoint the precise image you hope to express. Type not only presents the basic message, it can play a powerful role in the overall appearance of your logo and can actually create atmosphere. A chart of some of the more popular typefaces is included at the end of this chapter.

When deciding on a typeface for your logo, visit print shops or typesetting studios and look at their typeface books. They offer both the usual, functional varieties as well as a selection of unique typefaces that can really dress up your logo and subtly portray a specific personality such as dignified, fun, powerful, classic or cutting edge.

Have the logo and your business information (address, phone number, etc.) set in more than the one typeface so that you can see how they will look when printed. Also ask to have them set in both small (10- to 12-point for business cards) and larger (20- to 40-point for letterhead) versions. Once typeset, you will be able to make a final decision about which typeface suits the image you want to project.

Typesetters generally have a minimum fee based on the amount of time they spend on a job, which can vary from $15 per hour in a small city to $50 per hour in a business area, as high as $100 per hour in major metropolitan areas. That's why it's important to shop around.

> *Historically, in developing business names, simplicity has scored the highest points. The name you choose should be short, to the point and easy for consumers to pronounce.*

Word processing specialists or independent desktop publishers can also provide a variety of typefaces and formats at less expense. Since you will only be having a few words typeset, the time and cost required to set them in several different styles should certainly be affordable.

Business Cards and Stationery

The typeface and logo you eventually choose will be used on your letterhead; in your display and telephone advertising; on all promotional materials, including flyers, brochures, and announcements; on your sign; and on statements and invoices.

They will also be used on your business cards, one of the most inexpensive and convenient ways to inform people about your service or product. Once you have had cards printed, be generous. Give one to everyone you meet and always be sure to carry a supply wherever you go.

Most fast-print copy centers are prepared to help you if you decide not to design your own business cards and stationery. They have samples of business forms, letter-heads, and cards with various styles to choose from. Make sure that your company name, logo, address, and phone number are included where necessary. If you have a fax and/or toll-free number, be sure those numbers are included. When someone looks at your card or letterhead, it must tell them instantly who you are, what your business is, and how you can be reached.

Sample Typefaces

Arial
ABCDEFGHIJ
abcdefghij

Benguiat Frisky
ABCDEFGHIJ
abcdefghij

Bookman
ABCDEFGHIJ
abcdefghij

Bookman Bold
ABCDEFGHIJ
abcdefghij

Brush Script
ABCDEFGHIJ
abcdefghij

Chicago
ABCDEFGHIJ
abcdefghij

Eras Book
ABCDEFGHIJ
abcdefghij

Eras Bold
ABCDEFGHIJ
abcdefghij

Fenice
ABCDEFGHIJ
abcdefghij

Fenice Bold
ABCDEFGHIJ
abcdefghij

Futura
ABCDEFGHIJ
abcdefghij

Futura Light
ABCDEFGHIJ
abcdefghij

Futura Heavy
ABCDEFGHIJ
abcdefghij

Futura Extra Bold
ABCDEFGHIJ
abcdefghij

Garamond
ABCDEFGHIJ
abcdefghij

Garamond Bold
ABCDEFGHIJ
abcdefghij

Garamond Bold Italic
ABCDEFGHIJ
abcdefghij

Geneva
ABCDEFGHIJ
abcdefghij

Helvetica
ABCDEFGHIJ
abcdefghij

Helvetica Black
ABCDEFGHIJ
abcdefghij

Helvetica Condensed
ABCDEFGHIJ
abcdefghij

Monaco
ABCDEFGHIJ
abcdefghij

Palatino
ABCDEFGHIJ
abcdefghij

Palatino Italic
ABCDEFGHIJ
abcdefghij

Palatino Bold
ABCDEFGHIJ
abcdefghij

Park Avenue
ABCDEFGHIJ
abcdefghij

Stone Serif
ABCDEFGHIJ
abcdefghij

Stone Serif Italic
ABCDEFGHIJ
abcdefghij

Times Roman
ABCDEFGHIJ
abcdefghij

Times Italic
ABCDEFGHIJ
abcdefghij

Notes

Key Points:

_____

_____

_____

_____

Personal Thoughts:

_____

_____

_____

_____

_____

_____

_____

_____

Additional Research:

_____

_____

_____

_____

12

PREPARING A BUSINESS PLAN

Developing your business plan is the most important process you will undertake in your career as an entrepreneur, regardless of the size or type of business you have decided to start.

A well thought-out business plan will serve as a blueprint while your idea turns into a recognizable entity and as it grows into a stable and profitable venture. Too often we hear former small business owners say they probably could have made a success of their business if they had only known what to expect from the beginning . . . and that is where the business plan comes in.

Too many new entrepreneurs are unfamiliar with the importance of planning or consider themselves an exception and feel they can succeed by winging it or dealing with problems as they arise. Not so!

Every business, whether a large commercial or a small home-based venture, needs to analyze its potential, examine strengths and weaknesses and determine the future of the company. It works for the major corporations and it will work for you, especially once you become involved in the day-to-day operations of the business! Having a business plan will give you the freedom to follow the steps you have carefully laid out with regard to budgeting, the success ratio of a product or service, the hiring of employees and other growth decisions.

Advantages of a Business Plan

Once you have made the all-important decision to leave the 9-to-5 world behind, take the plunge and become a business owner, you must devise a specific statement that clearly outlines what you plan to do, when you plan to do it and how you will accomplish the short and long-term goals.

Not only will this keep you on track, it will serve as an indicator of your sincerity and knowledge to others when you go out to find start-up or expansion capital and as the foundation of your financing proposal.

The other advantage is that the actual task of putting your business plan together will help you define and clarify every step of your concept and, if done in a conscientious and objective manner, will point out potential trouble spots that can be addressed before they become a major problem.

If all the necessary components are covered, it will put your business on the road to profit. It is a sure bet that, down the road, if you find your business is not generating the income you had originally projected, it will very likely be because you didn't include one or more of the basic business plan requirements.

Not a Guessing Game

Like any other major project, preparing a business plan involves time and research. It shouldn't be a guessing game. It will be necessary to ask yourself some very specific questions and to answer them thoughtfully and honestly. The business plan is your foundation, so build it carefully to ensure that it works at optimum efficiency for your needs. And make sure it is typed so you, and others, recognize its importance in the professional scheme of your expanding operation.

An important aspect to remember is that your business plan is not cast in stone. In fact, one of the wonderful things about a business plan is that it invites change and revisions as your business changes. This makes it a companion in your success and, by reviewing it regularly, a partner in your progress.

The best way to approach your business plan is to take paper and pen and devote a few hours to coming up with some hard answers. Putting them down on paper will give you all the information you need to write the plan. Of course, you will want to condense your answers to fit into specific segments within the plan, including (in

Case History

Bernie Versadt started his medical claims service at home less than a year ago. He had been working as a file clerk at the local university and had decided he'd "had enough."

His aunt, Donna, was currently working as a doctor's secretary and was handling all the billing chores—and falling behind. The doctor agreed to give Bernie a shot at doing the billing if Donna would show him the ropes. After a short time, he was comfortably handling all the claims for the office. When he was offered a job doing claims for another doctor, he decided to go into business for himself.

"It's the best thing I've ever done!"

order of appearance) Concept and Feasibility, Legal Structure, Product or Service, Customer Base, Marketing and Production Goals, Personnel (your resume and Entrepreneurial Profile and those of any other key personnel), and Financial Statements.

It is advisable to start each segment on a separate page and to create a table of contents to place in the front. Be sure it is neatly typed, well-written and organized, and bound in a report folder to preserve it and give it a professional quality, especially when using it as a "sales" tool to convince lenders.

Key Questions to Ask Yourself

The first question you must ask yourself is: Why am I interested in this particular business? Probably to be your own boss and make money ... Independence and Income.

This answer is fine as a personal goal, but it isn't going to be good enough if you are planning to approach potential lenders for funding. They will want to see an overview of your business concept, why you are convinced it will be successful and where it fits in the scheme of similar businesses in your town or city.

The next question you must address is: What is my product or service? This may seem like a ridiculous question since you know your product is gift baskets or your service is catering, local sightseeing tours or whatever, but it goes deeper.

Your written response will include details about the service or a description of your product, preferably positive, and with a focus on why customers will be inclined to purchase from you.

Additional questions to analyze should include:

- Why do I believe there is a need for my product or service?
- How do I plan to develop my business over the next five years?
- How much will I charge to ensure value to the customer and profit for myself?
- Who are my suppliers?
- Who are my customers?
- What equipment do I need to start the business?
- How much inventory and supplies do I need for start-up?
- What will it cost?
- Who is my competition and where are they located?
- What are they offering and how can I improve my offer to attract customers?
- What changes are occurring in my marketing area which will impact my business in the future?
- What are my estimated sales figures for each of the next five years? (A "guesstimate" based on researching similar businesses in the area)
- How will I advertise and promote my business (including estimated costs of doing so)?
- How and where is my product going to be manufactured?
- What is involved in the production—materials, labor, costs?
- Where will my service be performed?
- What equipment is required for my service (costs for leasing versus purchasing)?
- What are other overhead expenses (rent, employees, etc.)?
- How many people will be involved in the business and what are their qualifications?
- If I don't have employees, am I qualified to run the business myself? Will I need outside assistance?

By talking with people in similar businesses, suppliers and direct competitors, as well as your local chamber of commerce, you will gather a great deal of information, both positive and negative, about your potential business. People love to talk about their success and, if you ask the right questions, their failure, as well.

Become an investigative reporter for a few days while preparing to write your business plan and it's guaranteed that you will obtain plenty of good, solid information. A SCORE representative through the Small Business Administration can also offer assistance, or give you resources that will help you develop a realistic business plan.

> *Show me a person with an obsession about succeeding and a solid business plan and I'll show you a good risk.*
>
> *Anonymous Loan Officer*

Trade associations, listed in reference books available at your local library, can provide you with invaluable details on industry facts and figures, such as the percentage of gross sales that should be spent on advertising, the percentage that is typically paid for rent in your particular business and how to price your product or service.

The final item to include in this section of your business plan, when and if presenting it for financing, is a personal résumé, designed to emphasize your business management experience, in general, and your expertise within the area of your chosen business, specifically.

Describe the job duties for every job you have held, including any special aspects that pertain directly to the business. If you cannot prepare the résumé, it is worth the $25 to $40 to have it done professionally.

Financial Statements

Once you have written your overview and description sheets, it is time to get down to numbers. This is the key to your business plan and, unfortunately, the area where many entrepreneurs get bogged down. But without an understanding about the numbers involved, you can never expect to be a good manager and really shouldn't be surprised if you run into money problems within the first year.

Again, utilizing the resources indicated above—chamber of commerce, trade associations, etc.—you will need to work up your financial pages to include the following components, which most lenders will want to see spread out for between one and five years.

• **Projected operating expenses:** Materials, advertising, salaries for employees or outside labor, and other expenses directly related to the cost of doing business.

• **Estimate of gross (before tax) sales revenue:** Based on research figures from trade associations and what the local market dictates, if the business is not yet operating or, if open, how many items or hours of service you plan to sell and the average price.

• **How you arrived at the figures for these statements:** Generally you would base your figures on assumptions made about the number of months of operation, estimated number of sales and the average amount versus the cost of each sale.

• **Cost of equipment and furnishings:** Get estimated quotes, whether planning to purchase or lease these items.

• **Cost of materials for production:** if applicable, or maintenance on equipment needed to run the business.

• **Additional operating expenses**: Rent, telephone and other utilities, business taxes and license fees, office supplies, even decorating costs and a category called "other" to provide a cushion for unexpected expenses.

• **Balance sheet**: Shows assets, such as equipment and operating capital you already have, and liabilities or debts and expenses (if the business has not yet started, this would be a personal balance sheet indicating your net worth; listing all possessions of any value plus cash, stock and other holdings minus all financial responsibilities).

• **Leasehold improvements**: If you are planning to rent a commercial location or redesign a room within your home strictly for business, estimate cleaning and restoration costs in this statement.

By investing the time and energy into this portion of the business plan, you will absorb the numbers into your consciousness and be able to recognize, at a glance, when your costs exceed your profit margin or when you are in a position to start making expansion moves.

If money matters are absolutely beyond your comprehension at this point, it would pay to hire someone to work along with you in developing the financial pages of the plan. There are business consultants and accountants who will probably charge you a substantial amount, or you can approach the accounting or business department of the nearest college and see if there is a qualified student available to help you.

No matter who you find to assist you, be sure to stay involved in the process . . . the discipline and hard work will guarantee success.

13

THE MATTER OF MONEY: FINANCING ALTERNATIVES

Starting your business without having sufficient capital is setting yourself up for problems from the very beginning. Undercapitalization is cited as one of the major reasons why businesses do not succeed, and this is the result of bad planning.

If you research and record all the goals, marketing data, equipment and supply requirements and financial needs of your venture before actually opening the doors, you will be able to see at a glance how much you need to get going and why you need it. That way, there will be no surprises and no reason that your business should suffer from lack of capitalization.

It is important to have the financial resources to cover all your preliminary planning and start-up costs, including expenses incurred to research the feasibility of your business and those required to set up shop, from equipment and supplies to advertising and utility set-up charges. You will also need a surplus to carry you over personally until the business becomes productive. The Cash Flow Statement and Projected Expense Charts provided in Section III will help you determine these expenses.

If, after drawing up your business plan (which is covered in the previous section), you find that your personal resources are not enough to open the business, there are other options available. The four most common methods include: a) starting the business on a part-time basis while holding a full-time job to cover expenses, b) taking on a limited partner, c) going to friends or family members for the money you need or d) applying for a loan through a commercial lender or the Small Business Administration (SBA).

There are, of course, pros and cons to each of these options.

Starting Out Part-time

Starting your business on a part-time or "moonlighting" basis is a decision that must be made based on the nature of the business. If you are planning to capitalize on your skills in upholstering, for example, you should have no trouble building up the business at night and on weekends.

It is perfectly feasible to start small, using your garage or home as your production facility and purchasing an answering machine for potential customers to leave a message while you are at your regular job. When you get home, you simply call them back to discuss prices and arrange a time when it is convenient to pick up the piece of furniture to be upholstered.

On the other hand, if you are planning to start a temporary help agency, for example, it would be in your best interest to go into it on a full-time, dedicated basis, as your potential customers are going to want fast results. They will call someone else if they are even slightly discouraged, such as getting a recorded message when they call.

Starting part-time will be practical in some businesses, but before exploring it as an option you must figure out if your limited availability will affect your credibility, if you really have the time and energy to work at a regular job and try to build a business (not to mention family responsibilities) and whether your ultimate goal is to be self-employed or just to earn a few extra dollars to supplement your base income.

Considering a Partner

Going into business with a limited partner who will put up the money you need while stepping into the background to let you run the business the way you see fit is a feasible idea. You must be sure, however, to have your lawyer draw up a precise partnership agreement that covers every eventuality. Partnerships are typically entered into with the best intentions and the unwavering belief that the business will be successful.

Since this is not always the case—and even if it were—it is a businesslike move to ensure that such aspects as decision making, distribution of profits and losses, contributions of partners and handling disputes and changes are outlined and approved by all the partners.

Friends & Family

The third option, raising capital through friends or family members, is probably one of the most often exercised methods. The advantage of getting a loan from a personal contact is that they know you, undoubtedly trust your ability to make the business go and won't require much in the way of substantiating paperwork, such as complex loan applications, financial statements, etc. In addition, you will most likely be able to negotiate a small interest rate on the loan.

The major disadvantage, according to entrepreneurs who have taken this route, is if the friendly lender decides they want to provide input on the care and maintenance of your business. This problem, however, can be eliminated by a "cards-on-the-table" discussion prior to accepting the loan. In other words, choose your investor carefully!

The second problem has to do with repayment of the loan. Even though you have a loose agreement in writing with your lender, because of friendship or family ties there may come a point when Uncle Bill needs that $10,000 tomorrow to take care of a personal obligation. You can't possibly come up with the money overnight, Uncle Bill gets angry and much of the family turns against you.

> *Money brings some happiness.*
>
> *But, after a certain point, it just brings more money.*
>
> *Neil Simon*

The flip side of the coin is if the business fails and you are unable to pay Uncle Bill or your old college pal the $5,000 he or she put up. These are unpleasant situations, so you must be sure in the beginning to think about the importance of the relationship you have with the potential lender, how the best and the worst of situations would affect the situation and whether you then could justify asking for money.

Commercial Lenders

If you are not able to, or decide against approaching friends or relatives for financial assistance, the next step is a bank, a savings & loan or a credit union. Before approaching any of these commercial lenders you must have carefully developed your business plan, which will include the following documents.

a) a resume or statement outlining your background and capability to operate the business, plus a similar statement about any key employees or partners in the business;

b) a statement of business and personal goals;

c) a description about the business, including research about the market for your product or service;

d) details on how the business is going to be structured (sole proprietorship, partnership, corporation, non-profit status);

e) a projection of profit and loss for a minimum of one year, which forces you to do your homework and investigate how similar businesses in similar locations are doing, and

f) an outline of how much money you need—and why—to keep the business solvent and to support yourself and your family for at least a year.

In addition, you will be required to provide a personal balance sheet which lists your assets, such as property, a car, etc., and liabilities like your mortgage payments, credit card debts, etc., and a credit application which outlines your personal financial history (so they can make a determination on your ability to pay back the loan). The lender will follow through by requesting a credit report from an independent agency, such as TRW, to help them make their decision.

The main thing to remember when applying for a loan with a commercial institution is that lenders aren't as concerned about how much money they loan as they are about how and when they are going to get the money back!

Approaching a Lender

Once you have your business plan and other paperwork prepared, decide which lending institution you want to approach. Certainly, if you have a stable record with a checking or savings account at your regular bank or S&L, that is the place to try first. Set up an appointment with the bank manager or loan officer to make your request and explain why you feel your business venture is worth their investment.

Be aware, however, that banks are more likely to provide you with a loan payable within five or ten years, as opposed to savings & loans, which are more interested in long-term loans, such as for mortgages. Credit unions operate in a similar manner to banks; however, you generally have to be a member. If you do belong to a credit union, it could be your best bet as they offer lower interest rates and can be more flexible in their determinations.

> ### Paying Back the Loan
>
> When you apply for financing, whether through a friend, relative, lending institution, a venture capitalist or some other type of arrangement, the burden of proof as it relates to repayment rests with you.
>
> No one would knowingly grant a loan to an individual or a business that they had doubts about. As a borrower, your responsibility is to show that you will be able to pay back the loan according to the terms agreed to. This can be done through a credit history that demonstrates a sense of responsibility.

If, for some reason, you do not want to run a loan through your bank, consider talking with other local small business owners. Very often, they can steer you to a regional, often independently owned bank or S&L which is empathetic to and supportive of new businesses. In that case, proceed as mentioned above and arrange a meeting with the manager or loan officer.

Present your case in a friendly, yet professional manner. Be realistic and honest about your needs. Do not underbid because of fear that you will not get a loan if you ask for too much. It is always better to start with a higher figure than you actually need so you have a strong negotiating edge.

In addition, most lenders have a pretty good idea about start-up and operating costs of new businesses and are much less likely to give you, and risk losing, a small loan for a business they know calls for more capital. They will be more willing to work with you if you are realistic and obviously knowledgeable about your needs.

If, after your first try, the answer is no, ask for reasons why you are being turned down so you can restructure your presentation. Turn opposition into a learning tool to redefine and polish your material and to develop new negotiating strategies.

There are always other potential lenders you can approach, and the law of averages dictates that you will get your loan if the idea is solid and it is apparent that you have researched the feasibility of starting a business in your particular area.

The SBA

The Small Business Administration (SBA) often goes where no other lender will tread and, as such, is a lender of last resort.

The SBA is a government agency that is well known for providing financing to entrepreneurs who have been repeatedly turned down by commercial lenders (which in fact must be the case before the SBA will consider backing you).

After your loan request with a commercial institution has been denied, you can file an application with the nearest branch of the SBA. It is a good idea to make an appointment with a SCORE (Service Corps of Retired Executives) representative, who volunteers his or her time to the SBA-SCORE program to advise new and established business owners. Your SCORE representative will be able to lead you through the complex paperwork required by the SBA before they make a decision.

In addition, the SCORE volunteers are usually straightforward, knowledgeable men and women who will walk through your business plans with you and offer constructive suggestions. Once the paperwork is completed, a commercial lender will make the loan under the SBA Lender Certification Program, knowing that the government is willing to insure it.

This option is recommended only after you have been turned down by three or more banks, because of the time factor involved in gaining approval and also because of the extensive follow-up reports required of SBA. It is, however, a viable option and one that has helped thousands of dedicated entrepreneurs realize their goals.

Venture Capitalists

Money is available to businesses that are already established and seeking working or expansion capital from groups of investors known as *venture capitalists*. These groups can vary from a few local businessmen with money to invest to major investment companies connected with large corporations or financial organizations.

Venture capital is not like a straightforward business loan. It is usually dependent on a minimum $100,000 investment and, therefore, is not suited to every business situation. Typically, venture capitalists are interested in companies that have a track record, a proven position in the market and a solid growth projection.

But, like a bank or other lending association, venture capitalists want to see a written business plan and a prospectus of future projections. They are looking at your background, the market, the kind of funding you want and your past financial record. Since venture capitalists are looking to earn from 10 to 15 percent on their investment over a relatively short period, they will want to spend a great deal of time talking with you and your associates, customers and suppliers.

Before considering venture capital, we advise discussing it carefully with an attorney who can help you investigate different groups and figure out the best investment structure for you and the organization you choose, and work with their attorney on drawing up an agreement that protects you, since many venture capitalists will want to become a part owner in your company.

This is an option to be considered only when your company is well-established and undergoing rapid growth pains and should be approached with great understanding of the situation.

Other Financing Options

Loan companies are an additional source of funding. However, interest rates are high and they will generally want to have substantial collateral, such as the equity in your house, on record before making a loan.

Insurance companies. Your insurance carrier may be willing to make an investment in your small business, using your insurance policy as collateral. Or, you may even have enough cash value in your policy, depending on the face amount, to provide you with substantial start-up capital. If this is the case, you will be required to pay only quarterly or semi-annual interest payments on the cash value you have taken out.

Factoring. In this instance, a factoring company "buys" your accounts receivables and advances you a percentage of the full amount due. This is a viable option for well-established service companies that work on a billing basis.

Co-signer. If you have a relative or friend who is already an established business owner or, at least, a homeowner with a solid credit rating, it might be worth your while to ask if they would co-sign on a loan application with you. Although you are still responsible for repayment of the loan, the bank is assured that, in the event you default for any reason, the co-signer will guarantee the obligation. It is often difficult to find someone who will do this, but again it doesn't hurt to ask, especially if it is a last resort option.

Starting Small

Even if you know your particular business is valid and that you have the ability to make it succeed, be certain that your business plan is realistic. If you have chosen to start a business on a grand scale but have minimal capital and little business experience, it may be best to begin a smaller, less elaborate operation at first.

You'll require less "seed money" and put yourself in a low-risk position while learning the ropes and seeing if you can handle all the variables of business ownership as it grows.

> *The journey of a thousand miles begins with a single step.*
>
> *Chinese Proverb*

Smaller businesses have proven to be a great way to learn the successful methods, as well as a vehicle for ironing out the many small details that are often overlooked until you actually start taking care of day-to-day situations. The profits you gain from a smaller venture can be used to expand or invest in bigger business ideas. And, an added bonus is that when you are ready to approach investors or lending institutions, you will be able to show them that you already have a solid track record and a working knowledge of business procedures.

What to Do When Asking for Money

A) *Be sure to ask.* This may seem like a gross statement of the obvious, but you would be amazed at the number of small business owners we talk to who never ask because they are afraid of being turned down.

Unless you are independently wealthy and pursuing your business as a humanitarian effort, it is unlikely that you are in a position to run your business and earn enough money to support you, your family and the operation—especially during the first year. Remember the old adage: It takes money to make money.

If you run a low-budget business you will probably get low-budget response. If you are determined to make it work, be sure you have sufficient capital to make it work the right way. Fear is often a factor: "I don't want to ask in case they say no." Well, that's the worst thing that can happen. But, if you persevere and are serious about your venture, someone will inevitably say yes!

And don't overlook friends and family; they can be your most ardent cheerleaders and supporters if you have given them reason in the past to believe you are responsible and determined to succeed.

B) *Know how much you need.* Lenders are familiar with the financial demands of business operation and will respect your request if you have obviously done your homework and can talk sensibly about your needs.

C) *Be direct and confident.* If you believe in your business and in your ability to make it work, others will be convinced. Never apologize for mistakes you feel you have made in the past and do not present the pathetic picture of someone who could make everything work if they just had enough money.

Simply present the facts, even if they include revealing an error in judgment you have made somewhere along the line, and assure the lender that they will be making a smart decision by investing in you.

D) *Think positively.* If you need $50,000, ask for $50,000. Never underestimate the potential to provide. Even if you are approaching family members, you may be surprised to find that dear Cousin Fred has a $250,000 nest egg socked away. Anyway, it is easier to negotiate and deal with one lender for a single amount than it is to keep paperwork and relationships strong with several, all of whom have contributed a little to the pot.

E) *Ask again.* If they trusted you once and you have lived up to the stipulations of the contract, ask again and that goes for commercial lending institutions as well as friends and relatives. A proven record is what it's all about and if you have established yours, keep it active.

F) *Know when to borrow.* If you have worked out your business plan and know you can survive while getting the business off the ground, start exploring your financing options ahead of time. Don't wait until the last minute; this will force you to act frantically and could put you in the position of accepting a less than favorable situation. The same theory applies if your business is already established. By examining your financial position on a regular basis, you will be able to project how much you will need at a given point for expansion purposes. Be prepared.

G) *Don't borrow if it is not necessary.* Many businesses can be started for under $500. This is called "starting on a shoestring." Services, for example, often rely strictly on the owner's knowledge and expertise and can be set up quickly and inexpensively.

If this is the case with the business you have in mind, then try to avoid borrowing capital. It can be an expensive and timely proposition. In addition, if, after a projected period of time, the business is showing the kind of profit you can work with while growing, then the smart decision is to utilize the funds and put them back into the operation.

Establishing Credit

Is it possible to get a loan even if you have never established credit? Yes, it is. Many people in this country still prefer to pay cash, rather than incur high interest charges on loans or credit cards. They can still qualify for a loan based on personal assets or by having a friend or relative with a good credit rating who is willing to co-sign. This puts the obligation on the co-signer, so be sure the terms of the loan are clearly spelled out in a written agreement to the satisfaction of everyone involved in the transaction.

However, if your personal assets are minimal and you cannot find a co-signer, the best bet is to put off starting the business for four to six months while you establish credit. The best place to start is with a major department store such as Sears or J.C. Penney's.

They issue credit cards based on a very simple examination of your income and employment history. Charge about $100 worth of merchandise when you receive the card and pay it off according to the schedule provided. Within a few months, you will have proven yourself to be credit worthy, which will greatly improve your chances of getting a loan from a lending institution.

Another way to establish credit—and credibility—is to open a checking account at the bank you have decided to approach for a loan. They generally require a minimum deposit of between $50 and $100. Make it a point to meet the branch manager and/or the loan officer and to establish an ongoing relationship with them by stopping by to say hello when you are in the bank.

Within a few months, apply for a small personal loan, working with your new acquaintance, of course. Make your payments according to the prearranged schedule. Then when you are ready to request a more substantial amount of money to cover your start-up expenses, you will be recognized as a customer with a loan history at that institution.

14

RECORD-KEEPING: YOUR BUSINESS LIFELINE

The motivating factor in any business is profit, which can be explained as the money left over after all the bills, for everything from supplies to rent and salaries to taxes, are paid.

Building a profitable business is not something that can be left to chance; it must be planned and a systematic method of record-keeping must be developed to help you control income and expenses.

You should expect that during the early days of your business, your profits are going to be minimal as you become established. But it is possible, with even simple record-keeping procedures, to prepare yourself for lean periods and control day-to-day expenses to ensure that you are, at least, breaking even. In addition, financial records are required for tax purposes and dealing with them systematically can eliminate an incredibly overwhelming task at tax time.

Record-Keeping Can Be Simple

Some people cringe at the thought of record-keeping or feel it is a waste of valuable time. Usually, these attitudes are based on a lack of knowledge and the feeling that it is an overwhelming task. There is, however, no other way to analyze your cash flow and make sure you are pricing products or services high enough to realize a profit.

In actuality, record-keeping is not such a complicated process. If you have ever balanced a checkbook or planned a household budget, you have basically done several of the same steps necessary when implementing a bookkeeping system for your business. And the good news is that keeping your records does not have to be either complicated or time-consuming.

We know of entrepreneurs who opt for total simplicity by using the "shoebox" method—every sales record, receipt for expenses and bank statement gets tossed into a box. This system has two distinct drawbacks. One may not become apparent until tax time, when you attempt to wade through the paper to prepare your tax return. (If you hire an accountant to do your taxes, it shouldn't come as a surprise if an additional "combat fee" has been added to the bill.)

> *Goals are dreams with deadlines.*
>
> *Diana Scharf Hunt*

The other, more critical drawback is that it is virtually impossible to maintain an accurate picture of your financial situation when you stockpile, rather than record, business transactions. In order to understand your cash flow, it is important to be able to see what monies have come in, what you have paid out, current balances and outstanding debts.

In fact, you should be able to answer the following questions with just a quick review of your records:

- What was my income last year (week or month)?
- What were my expenses?
- How do income and expenses compare with last year (week or month)?
- What was my profit (or loss) last year (week or month)?
- Where can I cut back on expenses?
- Who and how much do I currently owe on outstanding debts?
- Who owes me money and how much?
- What are my assets, liabilities and net worth?
- Is my inventory in line with demand?
- How much cash do I have available?
  How much credit?
- Am I able to pay myself this month (week)?
- Are my figures in line with projected financial goals?

The primary documents that you need to be able to answer most of these questions are a Cash Journal, a Balance Sheet and a Bank Reconciliation. A simple single-entry system, as indicated on the following pages, in which to record disbursements (cash paid out) and receipts (cash taking in) forms the base of your record-keeping.

Double-Entry Bookkeeping

Your accountant will probably utilize a double-entry system, which involves recording each transaction twice: once as a debit (on the left column of the ledger) and once as a credit (the right column of the ledger). For example, if you were to sell a product for $100, the transactions recorded in a double-entry system would be as follows:

The $100 would be written as a credit in your Sales account, since merchandise is going out of the business and $100 would be recorded as a debit in your Cash account since money was coming into the business.

This is a complex and time-consuming process that is often best left to an accountant, as he or she will need the information to create a monthly Trial Balance and other financial statements, including your year-end tax reports.

Single-Entry Bookkeeping

You can, however, have your accountant's office set up a simple single-entry system for you which will tie in directly with their requirements. Or, check out the standardized bookkeeping systems, which provide all the necessary forms and documents in a bound book, stocked by stationery stores.

One of the most widely accepted, ready-made systems is the Dome Simplified Monthly Bookkeeping Record. It contains forms for recording monthly income and expenses, summary sheets from which you can create a Balance Sheet and listings of legal deductions for income tax reporting. Instructions are included.

In addition, the trade association for your field should be able to provide you with systems developed exclusively for use in the industry, which you can use "as-is" or adapt according to specific circumstances within your business.

The final method is to purchase a Cash Journal book and set up your own monthly system, as outlined below for Office Assistance, a small typing service, which has been operating for one month. Any of the above mentioned methods are acceptable, as long as you understand the entry process and can "read" the results.

Make Record-Keeping a Daily Task

The easiest way (short of paying someone else) to be sure your records are kept up-to-date is to incorporate the task into your daily or weekly routine. Many small business owners make it a habit to enter their sales, expenses and other financial information at the end of each working day. It keeps them continually aware of their financial situation and ensures that there will never be any unexpected cash-flow surprises. The process probably takes no more than 15 minutes for normal transactions, but will save hours of pencil-pushing and frustration down the line. And, more important, you'll know where you stand financially.

Setting Up the Books

Using Office Assistance, a secretarial service, as an example, we can examine the various elements required for basic record-keeping duties.

Bill Miller, president of Office Assistance, has been in business for one month. Two months ago, he opened a new business bank account with $10,000, his start-up capital from a personal savings account.

At the same time, he rented a small office in a downtown building for $350.00 a month, but had to pay first month rent and a deposit of the last month's rent, for a total outlay of $700.

> ## Debit & Credit in Bookkeeping
>
> ### Debits include
> - Cash receipts
> - Purchases
> - Expenses, such as rent and wages
>
> ### Credits include:
> - Cash payments
> - Sales of services or merchandise.
> - Earnings, including interest earned

His fictitious name statement, which he got approved through the local county clerk's office, ran $10.00 and publishing it in a regional newspaper cost $45.00.

The initial month's lease and a deposit on a state-of-the-art typewriter cost him $275.00, plus $50.00 for a maintenance agreement. However, he will own the $2,000 typewriter when his payment schedule is completed.

He found a brand new calculator at a garage sale for $25.00 and is going to use a desk, table, lamp and chairs brought from home (value $350.00) to decorate the office. Phone installation was $150.00, but he purchased a two-line telephone for $79.50.

An artist friend designed his logo and letterhead on a computer for only $25 and a $6.95 lunch. He had his stationery ($35.00), business cards ($60.00) and brochures ($23.50) produced through a local copy shop for a total of $118.50.

A 2 x 2 inch display ad in the local newspaper cost him $370.00 for a week, and he is planning to mail 100 of his brochures to local businesses selected from the phone book. Stamps: $25.00 for the mailing. Office supplies, including typing paper, staples, paper clips, etc., set him back $45.00. A journal for record-keeping cost $7.95.

He purchased a packet of invoices for $5.95 and, during the first month, has billed and been paid $700.00. However, he has two accounts who still owe him a total of $400. Bill dutifully records information in his cash journal at the end of each working day. He uses source documents, including his checkbook register, receipts from cash purchases and billing invoices as the basis for his entries. The two pages following are for May (prior to opening the doors of his business) and June (his first actual month in business).

Office Assistance
Cash Journal for May

Date	Check # Invoice #	Detail	(Debit) Expense	(Credit) Income
5/1	100	Rawlins Real Estate (Rent & dep)	$700.00	
5/5	101	County Clerk (Fictitious Name)	10.00	
5/7	102	The Herald (publishing FNS)	45.00	
5/9	103	Ed's Keyboards (IBM 1-mo. & dep)	275.00	
5/9	104	Ed's Keyboards (Maint. agreement)	50.00	
5/12	105	Mary Smith (Calculator purchase)	25.00	
5/18	106	Telephone company (line installation)	150.00	
5/20	107	Phone Store (2-line phone)	79.50	
5/22	108	Ray Brown (logo design)	25.00	
5/24	Cash	The Hungry Dog (lunch/Ray Brown)	6.95	
5/28	109	The Copy Spot (brochures, cards, etc.)	35.00	
5/29	110	The Herald (advertising)	370.00	
		Total Income & Expense (May)	**$1,771.45**	**$0.00**

Office Assistance
Cash Journal for June

Date	Check # Invoice #	Detail	(Debit) Expense	(Credit) Income
6/4	111	U.S.P.O (Stamps for mailing)	$ 25.00	
6/6	112	Office Stationers (supplies, invoices, etc.)	58.90	
6/7	A1	W. Smith		$ 62.50
6/8	A2	Art Association		112.50
6/9	A3	T. Williams		22.00
6/9	113	Judy Miller (typing fee)	100.00	
6/10	A4	Bank of Cutterville		75.00
6/10	A5	WKTR-FM		120.50
6/13	A6	J. Johnson		43.50
6/15	114	Rawlins Real Estate (rent)	350.00	
6/15	A7	C. Lewis		73.50
6/15	A8	R. Swell		90.00
6/16	115	Judy Miller (typing fee)	100.00	
6/19	A9	W. Smith		52.50
6/23	116	Judy Miller (typing fee)	100.00	
6/26	117	Phone company (bill)	15.90	
6/27	A10	K. Black		48.00
6/30	118	Judy Miller (typing fee)	100.00	

Total Income & Expense (June) $765.90 $700.00

Bill's expenses for May and June were $2,537.35. Of course, part of that is for start-up expenses, such as deposits on his rent and typewriter, installation costs and one-time fictitious name filing and publishing. His income for the first month was $700. By deducting his expenses from his income, he can see that, at the moment, his business is showing a loss of $1,837.35.

Although Bill has been in business only for a month, he is curious about his company's financial worth and decides to work up a balance sheet to get the answer. The calculation, as indicated in the following example, is the amount owned (assets) minus the amount due to creditors (liabilities) which equals his worth.

Balance Sheet as of June 30

Assets		Liabilities	
Cash on hand & in bank	$ 8,162.54	Ed's Keyboards	$ 1,725.00
(Capital balance & June Income)		*(Balance on IBM)*	
Office Equipment	2,104.50	Unpaid rent *(July)*	350.00
(includes full value of IBM		Taxes *(estimated)*	75.00
even though not paid off)			
Office Furniture	350.00		
Accounts Receivable		**Liabilities**	**$ 2,150.00**
(outstanding invoices			
for work already done)	400.00		
Total Assets	**$11,017.04**	***CAPITAL**	**$ 8,867.04**
		Total Liabilities	$11,017.04

The figure Bill is most interested in is the *CAPITAL amount in the Liabilities column. This is the amount remaining after what Bill owes is subtracted from his current assets and is what his business is worth at the end of June. In other words, if he decided to try to sell his business right now, he could realistically ask that amount as a sales price. Of course, Bill probably wouldn't get that amount because he has not yet become established enough to warrant someone buying the business, unless they were looking for a "turnkey" operation—in other words, a business they could just walk into and get going immediately.

This information is valuable when Bill goes to apply for expansion capital or for credit on future purchases he plans to make, i.e., a photocopier, a computer and new furniture. His balance sheet will change each time he prepares it (probably quarterly in the future) as business increases bringing in more income and reducing his debts.

> *Money is a sixth sense which makes it possible for us to enjoy the other five senses.*
>
> *Richard Ney*

In the meantime, the Balance Sheet gives Bill a tool to use when comparing the financial standing of his business this month against future months and years. It also keeps him current on what he owns, whom he owes money to and his major sources of income.

The same procedure is used in developing a personal balance sheet, which possibly would be needed to establish credibility when applying for a loan. Assets would include furniture, automobiles, jewelry, your home and other tangibles, while liabilities would consist of outstanding loans and other major debts.

Bank Statement Reconciliation

Another important step that Bill must handle monthly is reconciling his bank statement against his checkbook register. He simply marks off the checks in his register that have cleared per the statement and the deposits which have been credited, and deducts any service charges for the previous month from his balance.

Bill then adds up all the outstanding checks—those listed in his register which have not cleared by the closing date indicated on the bank statement—and deducts them from the balance indicated on his bank statement. He adds up any deposits which have not yet been credited to his account and then *adds* them to the balance, as indicated below.

Balance per bank statement	$ 7,953.44
Plus: Deposits not credited	+ 325.00
Minus: Outstanding checks	- 115.90
New Balance	$ 8,162.54

The new balance figure should match that listed in his checkbook register and, in this case, it does. If, however, the statement and the register did not reconcile, Bill would have a customer representative at the bank review his statement and banking activity for the past month.

Pricing Your Medical Services

Tricky for Transcription

Pricing for medical transcription can be tricky business, especially with current healthcare industry changes and the expectations of some doctors or other providers that you may have as clients. The most common way of charging for medical transcription is by the "line count"—a set price for every typed line contained in a report. Another way of billing, which is gaining popularity for those dealing with digital dictation systems, is to charge "by the minute." Let's look at each of these.

By the Line

Currently most transcription is priced on a "per line" basis—meaning you get paid a set price for each line of text you type. What becomes tricky is that the number of characters (letters, numbers, symbols, etc.) per line can range from 65 to over 110. As you can see, if you have a flat rate of $.10 per line, you may be doing a lot more work for less money.

For example, say you transcribe one report that contains 5,000 words or roughly 35,000 characters. At 75 characters per line, that adds up to about 467 lines or $46.70 dollars. But if the doctor insists on 100 characters per line, you end up with only 350 lines and a gross profit of $35.00 dollars—a $16.70 difference for the same amount of work!

According to the American Association for Medical Transcription (AAMT), the character has been the preferred unit for measuring the productivity of medical transcriptionists since 1983. However, with more and more dictation being stored on digital dictation systems, many transcriptionists are adopting fractions of time for billing and production tracking.

By the Minute

This change is solving some of the problems that can occur from line count-based fees. A digital dictation system will measure the length of each report to the 10th or 100th of a minute. By billing per minute, it will be up to the doctor to make sure his dictation is clear and concise, because the longer he takes, the more it will cost. The current average rests between $1 and $4 dollars per minute, and the average dictation for an office visit is about 3 to 5 minutes. A doctor who sees 15 patients in a day may generate upwards of $150 per day—a set amount regardless of how many or how few words. This method of billing does away with any problems arising from "characters per line" as mentioned above.

You are a service provider so your billable time is exactly that—billable time—a kind of billing that is universally understood. Just as the phone company bills for time without regard to how many words or pauses are contained in each conversation, you get paid for the total length of time of the dictation.

According to transcription authorities, the two most compelling reasons to measure dictation by the minute of recorded dictation time are that: a) doing so gives administrators an accurate unit of measurement for budgeting future transcription expenses and; b) instead of allowing a dictating physician's poor dictation habits to devalue a medical transcriptionist's skills, measuring productivity by the minute of recorded dictation time puts the penalty fees for poor dictation right back where they belong: on the shoulders of the physician.

This avoids a medical transcriptionist's productivity suffering from time lost trying to figure out what a doctor with poor dictation is saying; time lost rearranging a document that a doctor dictated out of order; time lost looking up information that should have been dictated by the doctor; and time lost because a doctor miscoded a report and the medical transcriptionist had to start the report all over again.

Setting Your Transcription Price

What you price your services at will depend largely on your speed, knowledge and experience. It's recommended to start at $.05 per line if you're just starting out and your skills need work. If you have some experience and can type quickly and accurately (60+ words per minute) $.07 up to $.10 per line should be considered.

The standard starting rate based on minutes of dictation is approximately $1.00 per minute. After building more experience and knowledge you should be able to get $2.00 per minute for your transcription services. The Dictaphone company (makers of analog and digital transcription machines) recommends $1.30 per minute as a going rate for starting transcriptionists.

If you are in an area, or are dealing with a provider, that normally pays by the hour, the going rate tends to start at $7.50 up to $10.00. Pricing your services this way can put you at risk though; some providers require a minimum line count per hour or per day (sometimes 1200 lines per day) which can work out to less than $.05 per line.

Speed Is the Key

No matter how you price your services, your incentive will rest in your ability to transcribe quickly and accurately: if you type more lines in a day or type more minutes of dictation, speed equals profit.

You can figure out your hourly wage based roughly on your typing speed. Let's say you type 50 words per minute and average typing 50 minutes for each hour. So in an eight hour day you will end up transcribing 20,000 words (8 hours x 50 minutes x 50 words = 20,000 words). This translates to about 140,000 characters or 1867 lines. And at $.10 per line that works out to $186.70 dollars for the day or $23.34 per hour ($186.70 ÷ 8 hours = $23.34). Typing 75 words per minute brings your hourly wage to about $35 dollars; 100 words per minute can net you $46.68 or over $300 per day!)

There are also other ways to increase your speed without actually typing. Some of these "tricks" include software programs like PRD+, and Fast Forward or macro programs built into your word processor. These programs will automatically fill in the rest of a word that you start to type—leaving you to only hit the "return" key to enter it. This can increase your typing speed and productivity up to 50%. (We'll go more in depth in the Equipment section on how these programs work).

On average, most mediocre typists can make $30,000 per year without working too hard. That's not too bad considering they worked when and where they wanted and at a speed they were comfortable with.

Your Claims Rate

Setting your rates for medical claims business is fairly straightforward. Most medical claims services charge by the claim. Depending on your area, you will be able to charge $3.00 to $5.00 per claim filed. It is common to also charge a one time set up fee of between $100 to $500 depending on the number of patients covered by the practice. This takes care of all your preparatory data setup (patient info, coding, billing charges, etc.). You may be looking at the $500 as a decent amount, but consider this: most one-person, full-time medical billing operations can make $50,000 to $70,000 per year!

Other services that you will charge for include rejected claims. Many providers have a serious problem with rejected claims that were never refiled with the clearing house. The total could be as much as $50,000 to $75,000. You can go back 90 to 364 days, and with some carriers even further, to refile these claims. On average you can charge 10% to 20% of what is collected.

As a full-service billing management company, you will provide all accounting functions plus their claims processing. These services generally include preparing monthly statements, handling receivables, posting payments, generating reports, follow-up letters and collection notices. Typically, you charge a percentage of the monthly collected billing. This percentage ranges from 8% to as much as 15%.

The Bottom Line

As you can see, there is no exact standard rate—let alone pricing method. Once you have set your prices and have a few clients, by incorporating time saving devices to increase your productivity, you will see your income and profits rise.

Pricing in General

One of the toughest problems that small business owners face is establishing prices that, on one hand, the market will bear while, on the other, will cover overhead and guarantee a profit.

Often new business owners give the business away to get sales, but this is not an advisable practice. Realistic pricing indicates your confidence in what you are selling, and if you value your service, so will the customer.

Today's consumer realizes that they can't get something worthwhile for nothing, so don't be afraid to establish prices that will work toward your profit goals.

Pricing Guidelines

Several factors must be taken into consideration when setting prices:

a) **The cost of goods sold.** In the case of a retail or wholesale operation, this is the amount originally paid for the goods, while for a manufacturer, it involves the cost of producing the goods. In the case of a service business, overhead expenses and equipment costs must be taken into account.

b) **The nature of the product or service.** Uniqueness and demand come into play here. In the case of goods with a stable level of demand, such as bread or auto repair, the raising or lowering of prices will have little effect. However, when demand is high for goods that are hard to get, the price can realistically be set anywhere the owner wants.

c) **The competition.** Recognize what your competition is charging, for often this will guide pricing within a certain region. However, if a competitor is charging what you feel is an unrealistic price—either more or less—for a product or service, you owe it to yourself to find out why. Then set your prices according to all of the factors outlined here.

Even if they are higher than the competitor's, consumers will pay the price if you can offer an advantage, such as a friendly atmosphere, convenient hours or some other benefit not provided by the competition.

d) **Company policy.** This encompasses a number of things, including your location, your position in the marketplace, the additional services offered and takes into account your personal philosophy about business and your role in it.

e) **Market strategy.** Should you go for large volume at low prices or for low volume at high prices? That is the bottom line in considering market strategy. As a small business owner, you will likely opt for low volume and higher prices since the alternative involves having the resources, including labor, display room, distribution channels, etc., to move large volumes of product or perform major service tasks.

f) **Customers.** What will the market bear? In other words, what are your customers willing to pay for your products or services?

People expect prices that are fair; if you are planning to charge overinflated rates you had better be a top-notch salesperson or offer something so unusual that the price won't matter.

Although there are differences between establishing prices for retail operations, wholesale products, manufacturing and services, the basic formula for price setting is:

Labor + Materials + Overhead + Profit Margin = Selling Price

However, before setting prices on goods or services, it is extremely important to understand the concept of the Break-Even Point. Many small business owners operate on an overall profit-loss basis without realizing the importance of cost accounting. Being aware of such factors as your break-even point, markup and profit margin can tell you which areas of your business are profitable and which are causing a drain.

Understanding Break-Even

The break-even point is the minimum amount you must charge in order to cover all expenses incurred for the production and promotion of your goods and/or services without losing or making money. In other words, any income which is above the break-even point is considered to be profit and anything below it is a loss.

To find your break-even point, you must first total all of your operating costs, including materials and labor, equipment lease or purchase payments, advertising, utilities, office supplies and any incidentals such as gasoline, maintenance, postage, etc.

Generally, this is computed for a particular period of time, such as six months or a year. However, if your business is still in the early stages of operation, you can use the estimated figures on your projected expenses statement and "guesstimate" costs for materials and labor.

For example, the monthly expenses for a hypothetical cake-decorating business total $300 a month. You want to know what the break even point would be if you sell an average of 20 cakes per month. The calculation is as follows:

$$\$300 \text{ (expenses)} \div 20 \text{ cakes} = \$15.00$$

In order to break even, that is, without losing money or realizing a profit, you must charge a minimum of $15 for each cake sold.

The same process can be used to analyze the break even point on a weekly basis. First you determine your annual expenses by multiplying the $300 by 12 months, which would give you $3,600 per year.

The calculation to find the weekly break-even point is:

$$\$3,600 \text{ (expenses)} \div 52 \text{ weeks} = \$69.23$$

Therefore, you must earn $69.23 per week to operate the business without losing money and without realizing a profit.

Stay Informed

Knowing your break-even point is one of the greatest favors you can do for yourself as a business owner. It tells you how much you must charge for your products or services and serves as an invaluable tool in setting prices which will help you realize a profit.

Keep in mind, however, that the break-even point is a variable figure. Since it depends on production and overhead costs, plan to reevaluate periodically to make sure your prices reflect any changes.

Labor Costs

Labor costs, obviously, are the expenses incurred for the actual work done to manufacture or sell a product or to perform a service. Think of them as wages or salaries. Small business owners often end up working for free because they fail to set a wage for themselves. Despite the fact that you want to reinvest all of the income received back into the business for awhile, it is imperative that you establish a fixed salary amount for yourself when figuring operating expenses.

If you have set aside a survival fund to carry you through the first six months or so of operation, you may want to defer your salary until the business becomes solvent; however, you should still figure the amount into your expenses. Otherwise, you may find the prices you set are too low to justify making a profit from the onset.

It is much easier to set realistic prices from the beginning than it is to raise them later in an attempt to make up the difference. Remember, your time and skills are the cornerstone of your business, so think of paying yourself as you would any valuable employee.

Setting Retail Prices

If you were manufacturing items to sell at retail prices, without using a middleman, the following formula is a good basis to start with when establishing a selling price for your inventory of goods.

1/3 Labor + 1/3 Materials & Overhead + 1/3 Profit = Selling Price

---

You need a starting point. One place to start is with your labor costs. If, for example, the monetary value of your time and effort (labor) in producing an item is $6, you allocate $6 for material and overhead and an additional $6 as profit for a total selling price of $18.

If materials and overhead are costing more, you can: a) boost the price accordingly, b) review your expenses and find ways to cut back on material costs, such as finding a less expensive supplier or c) utilize a portion of the profit margin to cover the balance. Of the three options, b) is the best way to go.

You must also remember that when you are producing mass quantities of an item, your costs will be reduced because of price breaks on supplies and reduced labor costs per unit. You're then able to structure your selling price according to previously mentioned pricing factors, such as competition and demand for the product.

If you are starting a retail business which relies on selling products you purchase at wholesale, you may have some of your prices set for you by what the competition is doing or recommendations made by the wholesaler. However, there will still be items which you must price yourself.

This will involve understanding the principle of markup or gross margin—the difference between the cost of goods sold and the selling price, taking into consideration sale markdowns, shortages and discounts to employees. Generally, markup is stated as a percentage of retail price.

For example, if a manufacturer sells dresses to you at a wholesale price of $12.50 each and you sell them for $25, you would have a 100% markup (a 50% gross margin).

If you know the cost of goods and the average amount of markup you need to operate profitably, it is relatively simple to determine a price by using the following formula:

$$\frac{\text{Cost of goods}}{100 - \text{markup \%}} \times 100 = \text{Retail Price}$$

For example, if you purchased a gross of rubber ducks for a total price of $172.80 and had determined that you needed a gross margin of 36% to operate profitably, you would calculate the expected profit as follows, using the equation above:

$$\frac{\$172.80}{100 - 36} \times 100 = \$270.00$$

When you divide the Retail Price ($270.00) by the number of items (144: a gross) you get a unit price of $1.88, which you would probably raise to $1.98, depending on the market, to improve the profit margin slightly and provide leeway for markdowns during sales, etc.

Specialty items, such as antiques, artwork, imported goods and handcrafted items can be priced higher according to current value and what the market in your area will bear. They generally run between a 200% and 300% markup range.

Setting Wholesale Prices

Operating as a wholesale manufacturer greatly reduces your selling and administrative costs, because you are passing your products on to someone else to sell. Your price to retailers should thus be approximately 50% less than the suggested retail price.

In actuality, you are providing retailers with a discount because of their willingness and ability to promote your product.

The formula for wholesale pricing includes your profit margin + labor costs + expenses, which will be appreciably lower than for a retail operation because of savings on advertising, display equipment and maintenance, but which must include warehousing and marketing.

Pricing is typically more competitive at the wholesale level than at any other and is almost always the determining factor in whether your products are purchased or not.

Also affecting wholesalers are other wholesalers offering competitive pricing, middlemen buying large quantities at low prices and supply and demand factors.

As a wholesaler, you are in a position to vary prices according to the size of orders and your ability to negotiate with buyers. However, it is a good idea to develop a solid markup base from which to operate. This will allow you the flexibility to offer maximum and minimum prices for each item based on quantity buys.

Pricing is a crucial aspect of managing your business. Since you are in business to make a profit, it is important that you set prices which will result in the greatest income.

To do this, you must know what your costs are, or at least, have a solid idea of projected costs if you are still in the process of planning your venture.

By not setting prices that are too high or too low for the product or service you are selling, you will be assured of a favorable position in the market and a healthy share of the wealth.

Inventory as Investment

Ask 100 small business owners what inventory means to them and more than 90% will tell you it's the merchandise they keep on hand to sell to their customers or the materials and supplies stocked to produce goods or perform a service.

This is partially accurate, for inventory can and should be viewed as any supplies, raw materials or finished goods used to generate a profit in your business. But it isn't the response that a savvy business owner would give.

Surprisingly, according to a recent study conducted by a leading consulting firm, less than 10% of a group of 500 entrepreneurs interviewed spoke of their inventory in terms of the investment it represents; an investment that can range from 15% to 25% percent of total operating capital.

It is because of this "misunderstanding" that many small business owners often fail to incorporate good inventory control practices into their regular management routine. Although they keep an eagle eye on every penny going through the books, they may totally overlook the cash tied up in their inventory.

Controlling Inventory

Inventory control can be a very simple, straightforward task if you implement a workable system from the beginning—preferably even before you start ordering and receiving goods. You will find that time really flies when you are self-employed and it's easy to postpone such tasks as inventory control until, one day, you find yourself facing an overwhelming job.

Inventory control will give you valuable information about: a) Whether or not you are carrying too much or too little inventory based on, for example, items and prices preferred by your customers, or seasonal aspects, and b) whether you are realizing optimum economy determined by the costs of storage, taxes, handling and the investment per unit.

The ideal situation is to maintain an inventory that is profitable because it turns over (comes in and goes out of the business) regularly, lowering the cost of storing, displaying and insuring it.

There are several methods of inventory control that you can adopt, depending on your business. The main goal with each method, however, is to tell you how many items you have on hand and how many you need to meet your customer or production demands. It will also work toward lessening inventory shrinkage, which is generally the result of employee pilferage, customer theft, storing inventory incorrectly or maintaining sloppy records of items ordered, received and used.

You can tell how many items you currently have by making an educated guess, which generally only works for businesses having a small, visible inventory that is relatively predictable. An example of the kind of business which could probably operate efficiently with this "relaxed" form of inventory control would be a one- or two-person enterprise that monthly goes through, say, a box of invoices and similar supplies available for a minimum amount at the discount office-supply store.

Other methods of inventory control are the physical count, which should be done at least once a year anyway for tax purposes, or—the easiest and most efficient of them all—maintaining an ongoing record. The best idea is to incorporate the latter two systems; by backing up periodic physical counts with a perpetual record.

To set up your perpetual system, simply create a file card or inventory sheet set up in a three-ring binder for each item in your inventory. Across the top of the card or sheet, list the following:

a) item name and a code number, if applicable
b) a description of the item,
c) where it is stored,
d) the supplier's name, address & phone number,
e) unit price (i.e., $12.95/dozen),
f) your selling price (if a retail item) or percentage of gross price of completed product (if used for manufacturing) or service,
g) the date you place an order, and
h) the number of items and the date they are received.

Then, every time you sell or use an item, write it down and subtract it from the last balance. You should also indicate reorder number, based on when and by how much you must replenish your stock. The reorder number will be determined by such factors as: a) the minimum cost per unit available from your supplier, including quantity discounts, preseason specials and discounts for cash or quick payment, b) the delivery schedule, from the time you place the order until you receive it, and c) economic and social trends which can affect the way an item is perceived by the public.

For example, during a period of depressed or inflated economy, sales for leisure items typically drop. By keeping an eye on these factors, you can adjust your inventory needs accordingly and not get stuck with great quantities of items that you can't move.

After a while, you will be able to recognize at a glance which items are regularly used and which are simply taking up shelf space. When you reach this point, your ordering skills will become much more efficient and your investment in inventory will become a profitable proposition.

15

ORGANIZATION: TIME-MANAGEMENT TIPS

A recent survey of small business owners indicated that one of the qualities they felt contributed the most to their success was organization. In conjunction with this is the fact that time management and basic organizational seminars continue to be the most popular offerings in adult education catalogs and business workshops around the country.

Time is money! Because the small business owner is plagued by a unique set of problems, such as continual interruptions and overworking, it is vital to your success that you learn to manage your time and organize paperwork. This might sound rather simplistic, but you would be amazed at the number of small business owners who operate in a constant state of chaos.

Although we have seen a number of "A messy office is the sign of a creative mind" posters on entrepreneur's office walls, it is a good bet that the holders of these signs can recount story after story of missing checks, lost orders and misplaced files that totally disrupted the flow of business until they were located in a corner pile.

The survey respondents also stated that once they had learned to manage their time in both their personal and business lives and had set up guidelines for handling routine tasks, they felt more confident about accepting new challenges and making decisions.

The simple truth about getting organized is that it clears your mind for taking care of the nitty-gritty, profit-making aspects of being in business—production and promotion. For example, by allotting a certain place in your desk to hold customer files and billing information, you have made one major step towards maximizing production. Knowing that all the needed supplies and materials are located in one spot saves you valuable time and energy.

Making Time Work for You

Time management is the ability to take the hours we have available and use them to our advantage. Making lists of tasks to be done and giving them a priority rating is one of the best ways to avoid losing precious moments.

Keep a monthly calendar handy to help you keep track of major commitments, important dates and appointments. Try to avoid using it for notations of daily work in progress, carry-over tasks or other things that are best suited for inclusion on your daily and weekly lists.

There are several other ideas you can easily incorporate into your working lifestyle that will maximize your productivity.

• *Work smart.* Handle the jobs you find most difficult or cumbersome during peak performance time. If you are a morning person and find that making telephone calls to potential customers is one of your least favorite responsibilities, take care of them first thing in the morning when you are feeling fresh and energetic, and organize the rest of the day's tasks accordingly.

• *Set realistic daily goals for yourself.* Just because you are chief cook and bottlewasher, don't try to do everything at once. Learn just how much work you can accept and expect to accomplish in a given period of time and allow yourself to turn down work if it seems like it will be too much for you to handle.

• *Reward yourself.* When you are working alone, as many small business owners do when getting their businesses off the ground, there generally aren't many people anywhere around to support or praise your work . . . and everyone needs strokes! While it is true that a customer's praises are an indication that you are doing the right thing, you still need time to relax.

Treat yourself to a special dinner once a week. If money is especially tight, plan an evening where you go to bed early with a good book or do something that has absolutely nothing to do with business. And remind yourself that this is your reward for accomplishing certain goals for the week. It will help to keep your spirits high.

• *Don't procrastinate.* Don't put off doing tasks that must be done. If you constantly let some tasks slide because you don't enjoy doing them, you will soon find yourself terribly backlogged and unable to catch up. The effects of this may not show themselves until you are faced with a deadline and, at that point, you will discover that you are working at less than maximum efficiency, feeling tense and being hassled by small things. Even when business is slow and it seems that there could be little harm done by taking a day off to visit with a friend, be sure to complete required tasks before closing up shop.

- *Limit personal phone calls* during established business hours. Personal calls not only eat into productive time, they tie up the line when an important client may be trying to get in touch with you. The same holds true with friendly visitations. If you are self-employed, friends often feel that you are not really "working" and can stop anytime to chat. Explain that you will be happy to visit with them at a specific time and be sure to tell them why, so there aren't any ruffled feathers.

Obviously, there will be times when unavoidable situations, such as an emergency or an unexpected problem, arise. Try to take these inevitabilities into consideration by estimating how long a project will take and then adding a bit of extra time to give yourself leeway.

- *Delegate.* If you find that you absolutely cannot handle a certain aspect of the business, such as your own bookkeeping, for example, don't labor over the task—you will end up wasting a great deal of time and could make some serious mistakes. Admit to yourself that the task is just not a strong point and have someone else do it.

- *Learn to say no.* One of the hardest things for most people to do is to say "no." Even when we realize that, for example, helping a friend out on a special project will eat into valuable time, we often agree to do such things because we hate to say no. What we do is justify our acceptance by assuring ourselves that saying yes will put us in the position of meeting a lot of potential customers. The reality is that using that time to make phone calls or a sales call for your own business will probably result in a paying customer, not just a potential contact.

- *Minimize business meetings.* Before setting up a formal meeting, which can be very time-consuming, see if you can take care of the matter in question by phone or through the mail. If a meeting can't be avoided, make sure you specify a time limit to encourage people to get down to business. Another time-saving device for meetings is to work up an agenda that outlines exactly what has to be discussed to avoid idle chit-chat and unnecessary diversions.

• *Plan your time.* When you have to run errands, plan them for a time that is most convenient, such as in the morning when traffic is light. Plan to do as many things as possible in one trip, outlining the stops you must make so they follow a sequential order.

16

OPERATING YOUR MEDICAL CLAIMS & TRANSCRIPTION BUSINESS

As you can tell, medical transcription requires you to have the right equipment, attitude, accuracy and organization. This business can be easy to start and operate—giving you the convenience of working at home and making a decent living.

Setting Up for Business

As noted in the Equipment section, you should be comfortable with the supplies needed for this business—mainly your computer, software, transcription machine, printer, and modem (if applicable)—or you are becoming familiar with them, if you have had to purchase new equipment.

Your computer and keyboard are the main fixtures of your work space and should be set up directly in front of you. Your arms should hang comfortably and your wrists should be slightly raised above the desk. Fingers should be in standard typing position and the center of your monitor screen should be at eye level.

How's your chair? Most of your time will be spent sitting at your work area, so it's very important to have a chair that supports your lower back and will stay comfortable over long periods of time.

Your dictation machine should be within arms reach, either to the left or right of your keyboard, opposite your mouse (if you have one). You should be able to change cassettes or tapes without having to get up or move your chair. The footpedals that control the start and stop of the machine should be set on the floor so your feet can reach them comfortably.

Your phone should also be positioned on your desk, or table, and within reach.

A return or side table should hold your reference materials—standard, medical, drug, and specialty dictionaries along with any other books or binders you're using. (You don't want to keep books on the floor, that you have to bend over every few minutes to get at, or resting in the way of your keyboard or dictation machine, that you have to work around).

You may have other items that you need (pens, pencils, notebooks, etc.) and those should also be accessible, but out of the way of your primary flow of work.

Since your work area is where your entire business will operate, getting it laid out and keeping it organized, will directly translate to your bottom line—the faster and more efficiently you work, the more earning potential you have.

Assessing Your Abilities

There are basic skills that are at the core of the medical transcription business: listening, typing, proofreading and formatting. The more you know about each one, and the more time you can dedicate to improving that knowledge, will directly translate to success.

Your "Ear"

Medical transcription requires the ability to listen to dictation and understand what is being said. You may be concerned that you've had to ask people to repeat themselves on more than a few occasions. Not to worry—having a "good ear" is a skill that can be learned and will definitely improve over time as you transcribe more and more reports.

If you feel you need practice, use your dictation machine or a standard tape recorder and record a five minute segment of someone speaking on the radio or on television. Play back the tape and transcribe what you hear, leaving blanks for words you can't understand. When you are done count how many blanks are on your screen or page. Do a spell check on your computer or look up any words you're uncertain of in a dictionary. Count your misspelled words. Repeat this exercise with a new five minute recording. How did you do this time? Probably better and probably a little faster. You can see that with each transcription you do, it gets easier and you learn a little more.

Familiarizing yourself with each doctor's tone of voice, grammar and speech pattern will also improve your knowledge and better your skills. Speed will also come naturally as your business progresses—increasing your accuracy and income.

Your "Type"

Just like your listening skills, typing ability will improve with practice. The transcription exercise above will also help with your typing speed and accuracy the more you do it.

If you cannot type at all, you will need to learn at least the rudimentary finger positions and keystrokes. This shouldn't be too great a setback though. Many beginners become decent touch-typists in as little as a few days with continuous practice. Go to the library or a nearby bookstore for books on how to type, or enroll in an adult education class in your area. Another approach can be the use of typing software that will take you step-by-step through the basics and then test you on what you've learned. No matter which way you decide to learn, this is one skill that you can't do without.

The Proof Is in the...

It's one thing to be able to listen correctly and type up a dictated report, but without making sure what you've written is correct, your transcription is worthless. Proofreading your work is a necessary step to completing the job—it is the final touch that separates the novices from the professionals. How is your grasp of the English language? The computer will notify you if a word might be spelled incorrectly, but will you know if it's grammatically correct? Do you know the difference between its and it's? There, their, and they're? To, too, and two? Affect and effect...?

Having a basic understanding of sentence structure, spelling rules and grammar will be needed for you to make sure your transcription work is correct. No one was born knowing these things—they learned and so can you. Two of the best small books that will help you immensely will be Strunk and White's *The Elements of Style*, and *The Elements of Grammar*. Keep these references near you at all times in the beginning. After time, all the rules and exceptions will become common knowledge.

The Right Format

Each doctor or healthcare provider who becomes a client of yours will probably want their transcription to look a certain way when you submit it to them. Each report will need to be formatted for easy reading and quick scanning—you don't want to submit a solid page of text without paragraph breaks, indents or lists. But how these elements are used, along with abbreviations and medical terms, will be at the discretion of your client. Some doctors want every single acronym or initial written out, while others don't require that amount of precision. (See the samples later in this chapter for a good idea of how reports should look).

Working with Your Clients

Almost all of your clients will be doctors or medical personal who will be supplying you daily with dictation that will need transcribing. It's at this point that all your preconceived notions of how doctors act, speak, and interact should be thrown out the window.

You will be surprised to learn how bad many of your doctors' grammar, spelling, and ability to string complete thoughts together is. According to the medical transcriptionists we spoke to, deciphering and making coherent some doctors' dictation is by far the hardest part of the job. And on more than a few occasions, doctors have been wrong about their diagnoses.

What makes this task difficult is that people's lives can be at risk. A patient who comes in with malignant melanoma on his right arm is diagnosed and set for an operation—although the doctor has become confused and dictates that it's the "left" arm that will be operated on. This scenario has happened before. Your ability to check a patient's history and flag your transcription alerting the doctor to the mistake will not only prove your abilities as a qualified transcriptionist, but could also save a life.

This checklist will help you identify potential problems that may arise, helping you to keep an especially watchful eye on dictation and transcription:

1. Does the doctor have a history of deficient language skills or a problem keeping his mind "on track"?

2. Does the doctor dismiss your notes about problems without actually checking them?

3. Have you noticed more than a couple of significant mistakes? (Transposing body sides, confusing medical terms, etc.).

4. Does the hospital administrator, or primary contact, disregard your flags, or notes, of potential inaccuracies?

Your attention to detail and accuracy will be at the core of the work you do and will contribute to the lifelong success of your medical transcription business. It takes only a few extra minutes to proof your work and feel comfortable with the outcome—don't ever sacrifice your professionalism and attention to detail just to save a little time.

Step-by-Step

There is a standard work flow that most medical transcriptionists have in their day-to-day work. This will guide you through your own operation and show you how your day will run.

Doctors will usually dictate either throughout the day or save up all their dictation for the end of the day, relying on their notes and patients' charts. Your business day will begin by receiving this dictated material.

If your client uses standard dictation equipment (normal recorded tapes or microcassettes) you will need to physically get your hands on them. Some doctors will have couriers that deliver the tapes in the evening and pick up the finished transcription reports at the beginning of the day for yesterday's work or the following day for today's work. (The standard turn-around time for medical transcription is 48 hours.) This saves you the travel time as other transcriptionists are required to pickup the dictation themselves. If you are expected to pick up and deliver your work, you should budget and bill for mileage (currently around $.25 to $.40 per mile).

If you are fortunate enough to be using a digital dictation machine, you will have instant access from your home. (It will take an amount of equipment installation at your house, or place of work, depending on the system that you're using. This is usually handled by the provider or company that has hired you). This equipment works just like the standard tape format, except without the headaches of pickup, delivery and all those cassettes flying around.

Once you have the dictation, or have the ability to access it digitally, the transcription process begins.

It's recommended that you build a "template" or standard blank document that is formatted in the manner your client wants—font size, style, word and line spacing, headers, footers, etc. All of these options should be available in your word processing program and with exact instructions in the manual.

Start the dictation and transcribe away. You will be starting and stopping, rewinding and verifying as you go; this is normal.

Once you have reached the end of the dictation, go back and proofread what you have typed. Correct any spelling or grammatical errors you find. When that is completed, rewind the dictation and replay the tape as you read along making sure what is said in the dictation matches what is on the screen or page. Fill in any blanks that you may have missed the first time around.

Some of the things to check when proofreading your transcription:

1. Is the report formatted correctly: line spacing, headings, font choice and size?
2. Are all the blanks filled in or noted?
3. Are all the dates correct?
4. Are the headings in the report labeled correctly?
5. Are your pronouns consistent: he or she?
6. Is your verb tense consistent: has or had?
7. Words singular and plural: fibula or fibulae?
8. Are there any homonyms: to or two?
9. Consistent body side: left or right?
10. Is there any redundant information or repetition?
11. Are medications capitalized or not: Valium or aspirin?

Print out your transcription in its final form. Paper clip or staple the pages together if there are more than one. Flag any of the blanks that you could not understand, or any possible errors that the doctor may have made. Put the report and notes in a 9" x 12" envelope (or folder or other, depending on how the transcription needs to be returned) along with the transcription tape if applicable. Mark the outside of the envelope with the date, the case or patient number and the doctor's name. It is now ready to be sent back—either by courier or hand delivered.

Billing

As you decided your rates in the Setting Prices section, you will have to stay on top of your billing and make sure you get paid correctly and promptly.

Some of your clients will require an invoice or bill with each transcription you provide. Others will want an itemized invoice at the end of each week, two weeks or monthly. You will need to work out the billing method with each of your clients, and how your rates are structured (by the word, line, page or minute).

The Confidentiality Aspect

One of the main considerations in being a medical transcriptionist is to remember that what you transcribe is confidential. You may have noted that the sample contract in the Marketing section has a confidentiality clause.

If the information you transcribe is on a patient who is a celebrity, public figure, relative or friend, it is your responsibility to not mention this to anyone. It is both immoral and can be illegal to disclose to anyone, any name, diagnosis, problem or part of your transcription. Violation of this medial trust could surely end your career and even place you on the wrong side of a lawsuit.

Learning the Lingo

You will invariably learn how medical language is structured as you go. Most of the terminology is a basis of root words and various prefixes and suffixes. Terms are many times created by the doctor to describe a situation or condition; therefore, any understood combination qualifies as a medical word. Your medical references (American Medical Association Manual of Style, Dorland's Medical Dictionary, Stedman's Medical Dictionary, etc.) will define all the particulars, but here are some of the basics.

Some standard prefixes:

ab-	from, down
ad-	motion toward, addition to
de-	away from, off
di-	twice, double
hemi-	half
inter-	inside, inner
mid-	middle, center, in-between
normo-	normal, usual
ortho-	straight, upright, correct, right angle
para-	beside, near, resembling, accessory, beyond, apart from, abnormal
peri-	around, surrounding, encircling
post-	after, at the end

Some standard suffixes:

-able	capable or worthy of being
-acy	quality, condition, position
-ad	toward
-al	the act or process of
-ectomy	a surgical excision
-en	to become or cause to be
-er	akin to, reinforced by
-iasis	process or condition
-iatrics	treatment of a disease
-ic	of, having to do with
-ism	condition of being, act, practice, result
-ity	state, character, condition
-ode	like
-ory	having the nature of
-ule	little, small
-ure	agent, instrument of

Off and Running

It's a given that you will feel awkward as a medical transcriptionist in the beginning—you will still be learning and may get discouraged on occasion. Perseverance will help you through these low points, along with the knowledge that you are in a growing industry that will reward you with both excellent income and freedom of time.

Transcription Samples

A lot of your transcription will be in the SOAP format (subjective diagnosis, objective diagnosis, assessment and plan, or procedure) which is an industry standard. Here are some examples of office, lab and hospital transcriptions in the SOAP and other standard formats.

OFFICE PHYSICAL

I.

Date:	4/7/96
Patient:	SMITH, JOHN JACOB
ID#:	SMJJ2050
Doctor:	WALLACE, SUSAN R.

S: The patient presents for a physical. His main problem has been some pains in the neck, elbows and lower back. The back pain has been present for just a few days and is slightly worse with movement. He has had pains in his elbows for approximately four months. It is relatively constant, no extreme. It does tend to hurt when he supinates his forearm fully. He has also had some mild pain in the back. At one time, he was thought to possibly have cervical disc disease; however, a CT scan of the cervical spine was unremarkable. He has no other significant history. Social: He is a nonsmoker. Family history: His father does have some mild arthritis and also has hypertension and heart disease.

O: HEENT: Tympanic membranes are clear bilaterally. Nose and throat are clear. Neck is supple without lymphadenopathy or bruits. Cardiovascular: Regular rate and rhythm without murmur. Abdomen: Soft, flat, nontender, and nondistended. Bowel sound are active. He has some minimal tenderness in the right lower quadrant. Back: There is trigger-point tenderness. Lower extremities are normal to exam. He has negative straight leg raising in the supine position.

Laboratory studies were within normal limits, with the exception of his cholesterol which was 236 and his triglycerides which were 320. He is not watching his diet at all.

A: Strain of the lower back. I think this may well be due to his work as a clerk. He spends a lot of time at a computer keyboard.

P: He is to take the strain off of his elbows and lower back. I also gave him an instruction sheet on a low-cholesterol diet. He will try to follow this for six months, and we will recheck his cholesterol then. He asked if I would recommend taking niacin. I told him that it might have some beneficial effect and was probably relatively safe for him to take.

II.

Date:	9/15/97
Patient:	LOUISE, GERTRUDE LAMB
ID#:	LGL7120
Doctor:	IRVING, NICHOLAS J.

S: This is a 78-year-old white female with multiple complaints. She has a history of chronic sinusitis, esophagitis, a fibromyalgia-type syndrome, and depression. She complains today of continued problems with pain in the left cheek and preauricular area, especially in the morning. The pain gets very intense at times. She also has a great deal of postnasal drainage which gives her a sour feeling in her stomach. She also complains of some dizzy spells over the last few months, usually when she is working around the house. These are associated with some sweating and nausea. She has not ever had any loss of consciousness. She also complains of recurrent problems with constipation, especially over the last three months. She has been using Correctol. This tends to give her runny stools for a day and then she has constipation again the next day. She has tried taking Colace. This was not helpful.

O: General: She is a well-nourished, well-developed, elderly white female in no acute distress. She appears somewhat sad and tearful. HEENT: Tympanic membranes were clear bilaterally. Nose had some pale mucosa, otherwise clear. She had tenderness along the left maxillary and left preauricular areas, and some mild temporomandibular joint tenderness. Throat was clear. Neck was supple. Lungs: Clear to auscultation. Cardiovascular: Regular rate and rhythm without murmur. Abdomen: Soft and diffusely tender to a mild degree. Bowel sounds were active.

A:　1. Depression.
　　2. Recurrent sinus pain.
　　3. Constipation.
　　4. Esophagitis.

P: 1. She has been off Zoloft for a while, so we will have her resume that. There is no record in the chart of her ever having an adverse reaction to it. 2. Beconase AQ 2 puffs b.i.d. 3. For her constipation, I recommended using Metamucil or some other type of similar fiber, and increasing her fluid intake. She is going to make an appointment with Dr. Suess at his next opening, so that he can follow up on how she is doing with these changes. If she continues to have the sinus pain, we may need to refer her to an otolaryngologist.

HOSPITAL

III.

Date: 1/17/96
Patient: WILLIAMS, COLE M.
ID#:   WCM1000
Physician: PAUSCH, ABEL C.

HISTORY AND PHYSICAL:

History of Present Illness:
This is a 43-year-old black man with no apparent past medical history who presented to the emergency room with the chief complaint of weakness, malaise and dyspnea on exertion for approximately one month. The patient also reports a 15-pound weight loss. He denies fever, chills and sweats. He denies cough and diarrhea. He has mild anorexia.

Past Medical History:
Essentially unremarkable except for chest wall cysts which apparently have been biopsied by a dermatologist in the past, and he was given a benign diagnosis. He had a recent PPD which was negative in August 1994.

Medications:
None.

Allergies:
No known drug allergies.

Social History:
He occasionally drinks and is a nonsmoker. Denies intravenous drug use. The patient is currently employed.

Family History: Unremarkable.

PHYSICAL EXAMINATION:

General:
This is a thin, black cachectic man speaking in full sentences with oxygen.

Vital Signs:
Blood pressure 96/56, heart rate 120. No change with orthostatics. Temperature 101.6 degrees Fahrenheit. Respirations 30.

HEENT:
Funduscopic examination normal. He has oral thrush.

Lymph:
He has marked adenopathy including right bilateral epitrochlear and posterior cervical nodes.

Neck:
No goiter, no jugular venous distention.

Chest:
Bilateral basilar crackles, and egophony at the right and left middle lung fields.

Heart:
Regular rate and rhythm, no murmur, rub or gallop.

Abdomen:
Soft and nontender.

Genitourinary:
Normal.

Rectal:
Unremarkable.

Skin:

The patient has multiple, subcutaneous mobile nodules on the chest wall that are nontender. He has very pale palms.

Laboratory and X-Ray Data:

sodium	133
potassium	5.3
BUN	29
creatinine	1.8
hemoglobin	14
white count	7100
platelet count	515
Total protein	10
albumin	3.1
AST	131
ALT	31

Urinalysis shows 1+ protein, trace blood. Total bilirubin 2.4, direct bilirubin 0.1. Arterial blood gases: pH 7.46, pC02 32, p02 46 on room air. Electrocardiogram shows normal sinus rhythm. Chest x-ray shows bilateral alveolar and interstitial infiltrates.

IMPRESSION:

1. Bilateral pneumonia; suspect atypical pneumonia, rule out pneumocystis carinii pneumonia and tuberculosis.
2. Thrush.
3. Elevated unconjugated bilirubins.
4. Hepatitis.
5. Elevated globulin fraction.
6. Renal insufficiency.
7. Subcutaneous nodules.

PLAN:

1. Induced sputum, rule out pneumocystis carinii pneumonia and tuberculosis.
2. Begin intravenous Bactrim and erythromycin.

3. Begin prednisone.
4. Oxygen.
5. Nystatin swish and swallow.
6. Dermatologic biopsy of lesions.
7. Check HIV and RPR.
8. Administer Pneumovax, tetanus shot and Heptavax if indicated.

IV.

Date:	5/18/98
Patient:	HOWELL, CARL H.
ID#:	HCH2210
Physician:	CURRY, NORMAN P.

OPERATIVE REPORT PREOPERATIVE DIAGNOSIS:
Right foot infection.

POSTOPERATIVE DIAGNOSIS:
Right foot infection.

PROCEDURE:
Right below-knee amputation.

SURGEON:
Nancy Cartwright, M.D.

ANESTHESIA:
Spinal.

FLUIDS:
300 cc Ringer's lactate.

ESTIMATED BLOOD LOSS:
250 cc.

INDICATIONS FOR SURGERY:
This is a 70-year-old male with a history of insulin-dependent diabetes mellitus, coronary artery disease, chronic renal failure and heart failure who was initially admitted for congestive heart failure and nonhealing bilateral foot ulcers treated for years with debridement and whirlpool. The patient was readmitted for acute diabetic right foot. Recently his foot had been worsening. He had been using dry dressings. He was admitted and taken to the operating room for incision and drainage of his right foot and amputation. The patient's infection could not be eradicated from the foot; therefore, it was decided to take him for right below-knee amputation.

DESCRIPTION OF PROCEDURE:
The patient was taken to the operating room and placed on the operating room table in the right lateral decubitus position. After placement of intravenous lines and electrocardiogram leads, spinal anesthesia was induced. The patient was placed supine and the patient's right lower limb was sterilely scrubbed with Betadine and prepared with Betadine paint in a sterile fashion. The patient's right lower limb was draped in a sterile fashion after the application of a tourniquet to the right upper thigh. The tourniquet was not inflated during the case.

We first turned our attention to the foot and made a transmetatarsal incision with a 10-blade scalpel around the foot. We performed a transmetatarsal amputation at first. There did not seem to be bleeding or viable tissue at this amputation site, especially posteriorly on the foot. Therefore it was decided to carry the amputation up to a below-knee amputation. A fish-mouth incision was made at the midtibia, leaving more posterior tissue to form a lip for closure. Using the 10-blade scalpel, we cut circumferentially the soft tissue around the tibia and fibula, being careful to clamp bleeding vessels which appeared along the way. We cut through all the soft tissue muscle tendons and were careful to identify the peroneal nerve and the tibial nerve, and to stretch these as far down as possible and cut them as far proximally as possible so they would retract and not form neuromas. We tied off the major vessels, the tibial and peroneal arteries. After the soft tissue was removed, the tibia was cut with the oscillating hand saw approximately 3 cm proximal to the skin incision. The end was rasped away so there would be smooth edges. The fibula was cut with the hand saw 2 cm above this, and the end was rasped off as well to a smooth dry point. Hemostasis was obtained with the cautery, and also with Vicryl suture used to tie off some bleeding vessels.

The fascial tissue layer was closed with 0-Vicryl figure-of-eight sutures. After this, 0-Vicryl was used to bring the skin together by bringing the subcutaneous tissue above the fascia. The last layer of skin was closed with 4-0 nylon interrupted sutures. A sterile dressing and Ace wrap were placed over the wound. We also inserted a small drain into the wound. The patient tolerated the procedure well and was returned to the recovery room in stable condition.

LABORATORY

V.

Date:	11/13/94
Patient:	SPENCER, JAN A.
ID#:	SJA9805
Physician:	BLANCHARD, HENRY
Technician:	JOHANSEN, D.

ELECTRONYSTAGMOGRAPHY REPORT (ENG) CLINICAL HISTORY
This is a 43 year old with seizure disorder and recent imbalance with stair climbing.

The following examinations are performed with horizontal and vertical electrodes.

Saccadic eye movements are well organized in the horizontal and in the vertical directions. Gaze and fixation testing, including straight gaze, gaze to the left, gaze to the right, and gaze upward and downward, produces no nystagmus. The oscillating tracking test reveals well-organized horizontal pursuit movements to each side.

Bidirectional opticokinetic testing with peripheral stimulation produces horizontal nystagmus of appropriate direction with the targets moving to each side. The torsion swing test with the eyes closed produces normal direction-changing horizontal nystagmus. Positional head testing with the eyes closed and the patient in the head hanging, left lateral, right lateral, and sitting positions produces no nystagmus. Cold and warm water caloric testing of each ear produces horizontal nystagmus of appropriate direction.

SUMMARY
Electronystagmography within normal limits.

VI.

Date: 11/13/94
Patient: HIGGINS, DANA
ID#:   HD07000
Physician: LAWS, PETER G.
Technician: SULLY, N.

ELECTROENCEPHALOGRAM REPORT (EEG)
Age: 62. Patient is on Neurontin, phenobarbital, and Dilantin.

ANALYSIS OF PATTERN
There is a bioccipital rhythm, which is organized, of about 8 Hz. Frontal activity is a mixture of rapid and slow activity. Bifrontal spike and slow wave activities are noted, which have been noted in previous EEGs. High voltage delta slow waves are also noted intermittently in the frontal areas.

The spike activity noted does not generalize but spreads occipitally. Interictally, the EEG has some slow theta activity in the 5-6 Hz range. The spike and slow activity is not frequent but intermittently increases in frequency. Two episodes of every 1 second, lasting 4 seconds, are recorded. Otherwise, the spike activity appears between 2 minutes to 3 minutes in the EEG. The high-frequency delta waves are not as frequent. One episode lasting up to 5 seconds is also noted. No clinical correlation was noted with this EEG by the EEG tech or by the patient. The patient is not photosensitive.

IMPRESSION
Compared to the previous EEG, it is either unchanged or slightly better.

CORRESPONDENCE

PATIENT CARE PLAN LETTER TO HEMATOLOGIST

RE: McMahon, James

Dear Dr. Benrabi:

I am sending Mr. McMahon to you in regards to some leukopenia and thrombocytopenia. He was a previous patient of Dr. Stratton and evidently had some low platelets and white counts in the past. In February, he had a white count of 4100 with essentially a normal differential. His platelet count was 130,000.

We repeated his complete blood count recently. He continues to have no anemia, but his white count is now 2800 and platelet count is 109,000. Antinuclear antibody was negative. His blood chemistry profile did show a mildly low globulin at 1.7. Uric acid was slightly elevated at 8.7. Bilirubin was at 2. His retic count was 3 with an absolute reticulocyte count of 139.5, which is about double normal.

I have included the laboratory studies for you to review. His vitamin B12 level was normal at 282. He is somewhat reluctant to see a hematologist. I told him that you may recommend a bone marrow exam. At this point, he is feeling well and does not understand why he would nee to see another physician.

I appreciate your evaluation.

Sincerely,

Dr. Holloway-Klein

Operating Your Claims Business

Okay, you want to make it in the world of medical claims—let's get down to business. There are a few things you need to understand first:

1. This is a very easy business to start.
2. There are little or no overhead costs.
3. Day-to-day operations are a snap.
4. The profit potential in enormous.
5. Expanding the business is simple.

If it sounds like there is enormous potential in this industry, you heard correctly—medical claims is one of the fastest growing of the new high profit businesses.

Where to Start

You may want to jump right in and start a full-service management company (they make the most profit), but unless you already have some medical claims and accounting experience, there is a safer route to success.

We always recommend that people start their business with medical claims only and add the accounting, patient billing, or even transcription, later. Since medical claims is really at the heart of any healthcare business—the in-flow of money—it needs to be addressed first.

As medical transcription relates to carefully recording the words, medical claims is the art of capturing the numbers. To be successful in either form of medical billing—claims only or full-practice management—or medical bill auditing, you need to understand the general operation of Medicare, Medicaid and the insurance industry, and how to fill out electronic and paper claim forms. For this information you will want to familiarize yourself with some of the basics that the Health Care Financing Administration, or HCFA, provide.

The HCFA

The Health Care Financing Administration (HCFA) is the primary Federal agency responsible for administering the Medicare program and overseeing the Medicaid program. Combined, these programs currently serve approximately 72 million Americans who will receive $314 billion in benefit payments in 1997. As the nation as a whole "grays," the number of uninsured increases and the cost of health care services continues to rise; the Administration, Congress, and the health care industry will put forth initiatives to restructure parts of the national health care environment.

The HCFA generates the guidelines by which the medical claims industry operates—sending out modifications and new standards each year along with industry codes (200 new codes for 1996 alone) and forms (the HCFA-1500 form).

What Is Medicare?

Medicare is a federal health insurance program for people 65 or older, and certain disabled people, that is run by the HCFA. Social Security Administration offices across the country take applications for Medicare and provide general information about the program.

Medicare is divided into two parts: Hospital insurance (Part A) and Medical insurance (Part B). Hospital insurance covers the more immediate needs of the patient including hospital and nursing facilities, home health care and hospice. Medical insurance covers doctor and outpatient services, medical equipment and other services and supplies that Part A doesn't cover.

Generally, people age 65 and older can get premium-free Medicare Part A benefits, based on their own or their spouses' employment. (Premium-free means there are no monthly or yearly premium payments. Most people do not pay premiums for Medicare Part A.) Patients can get premium-free Medicare Part A if they are 65 or older and any of these three statements is true:

- They receive benefits under the Social Security or Railroad Retirement system.
- They could receive benefits under Social Security or the Railroad Retirement system but have not filed for them.
- They or their spouse had Medicare-covered government employment.

Medicare Medical Insurance (Part B) can be applied for by any person who can get premium-free Medicare Part A benefits based on work as described above and can pay the monthly Part B premiums (in 1995, $46.10 for most beneficiaries). In addition, most United States residents age 65 or over can enroll in Part B.

What Is Medicaid?

Title XIX of the Social Security Act is a program which provides medical assistance for certain individuals and families with low incomes and minimal resources. The program, known as Medicaid, became law in 1965 as a jointly funded cooperative venture between the Federal and State governments to assist states in the provision of adequate medical care to eligible needy persons. Medicaid is the largest program providing medical and health-related services to America's poorest people.

Within broad national guidelines which the Federal government provides, each of the states: (1) establishes its own eligibility standards; (2) determines the type, amount, duration, and scope of services; (3) sets the rate of payment for services; and (4) administers its own program. Thus, the Medicaid program varies considerably from state to state, as well as within each state over time.

To be eligible for Federal funds, states are required to provide Medicaid coverage for most individuals who receive federally assisted income maintenance payments, as well as for related groups not receiving cash payments.

This background information should help you to understand some of the terms and programs involved that are standard within the industry. Other private insurance agencies will have their own systems of eligibility and billing structure, but you will have to contact them directly for specifics.

An Industry Revolution

Medical claims is seeing some revolutionary changes come along that are taking this business into the 21st century— making it easier than ever to operate.

The entire business originated as a manual, clerical task that for most was a necessary evil. Secretaries, receptionists and medical staff were forced to sort through insurance guidelines, forms, patient bills and reimbursement checks trying to make sense of the whole process, and make sure they were receiving the right amount of money for the right procedures. Many providers were realizing a payment rate of only 70% on their old paper claims—losing an incredible $30,000 for every $100,000 that was billed!

Ah, but the advancement of computers and the simplifying of the process has brought forth a whole new industry in the form of electronic claims processing—this is where the money is!

I Sing the Claim Electric

Electronic claims processing (or medical billing) can be a very simple business to operate. Basically if you can read and type, you're in business. Your job will be to collect the provider's superbills or any other billing records and input the information directly into your computer. When you are through entering the data, you will send it instantly over the phone line to the clearing house for auditing and editing. Because of the low rejection rate of electronically filed claims (2%, as opposed to 25% to 30% for paper claims), you will be able to process more claims—and at about $2–$4 per claim, that adds up very quickly.

Your initial start-up will be a bit more expensive as an electronic claims processor, but the amount of work and speed at which it is accomplished, will earn you back the money invested in no time.

Sorting Out Your Skills

Since you will be offering your clients a service, your skills should be up to par with what's expected in the industry. The primary skills that you should have for this business are organization and accuracy.

Whether you're processing claims manually or electronically, you are the middle person between the healthcare provider and the insurance agency. You will be processing a large number of claims that will need to be documented, ordered and available for auditing or editing. Because of the automatic nature of medical claims billing software, these tasks are simple.

If you have to file paper claims, for whatever reason, you will need to manually handle each task—stocking claims forms, filling them out on a typewriter or by hand, making copies to keep on site and file, mailing finished forms to the clearing house, and being able to access patient information if there is a mistake or additional data is needed.

The Medical Claims Process Simplified

As we've noted, understanding the processes involved in this industry will be tantamount to your success. This is a general step-by-step work flow for the medical claims process:

1. A patient goes to a doctor or healthcare provider for treatment. Most standard procedures will be covered by their insurance company. Any non-standard procedures will need to be cleared by the insurance company for coverage, or by the patient's discretion.

2. After services are rendered, a doctor will write up what procedures were performed, medication used, or supplies utilized using a coded system. The patient's name or identification number and visit codes are written or printed out in a list showing all the patients for the day. This is called a superbill.

3. A medical claims person will take the superbill and fill out individual claims forms for each patient. Each claim form is either printed out and mailed or sent electronically to a clearing house for auditing and verification.

4. The clearing house will notify the medical claims person about any rejected claims, usually within 24 hours of receiving them. Claims are rejected if there are any errors or missing information. A rejected claim needs to be edited or completed and resent to the clearing house.

5. Once the claim is correct and verified, the clearing house sends it directly to the insurance company who will then pay the doctor or healthcare provider. Electronic claims are processed and paid within 7 to 14 days while paper claims can take as long as 3 months.

On average, 30 to 50% of all claims are rejected because of missing or incorrect information. Of these, almost all are the handwritten paper claims. Add on mailing, sorting, data entry and recording time and it becomes apparent why it takes so long for reimbursement for manual filing. But most important, medical claims people get paid according to each correct claim. And at up to $5 per claim, you can see how the speed and accuracy of electronic filing makes sense.

Step-by-Step

There is some amount of preparation work that will need to be done to speed up your processing job. This involves entering patient data (name, identification number, age, address, phone numbers, insurance carrier, insurance identification numbers, insurance coverage, social security number, family members, etc.) into your medical billing software program if possible. Having to enter this information as you go will obviously slow you down—limiting the amount of work you'll be able to process in the beginning. It's at this point that you should be able to realize how tedious filing manual claims would be—filling out this information every time you filed a claim—and how a majority of the mistakes get made. (You will usually charge a one time set-up fee for this—see the Setting Prices section for specifics.)

Your job will begin the second you receive your client's superbill. This superbill is generally a roster of that day's (or week's) patient visits, procedures, and billing information listed in columns by name, identification number, and diagnoses, procedure and insurance codes. From this superbill, you will be able to fill out a separate claim form for each patient listed.

Those Old Code Blues

One aspect of filling out claims involves learning how to enter two special coding systems that doctors are required to use on the claim form. These codes indicate the diagnosis and the procedures that are performed on each patient. Entering these codes is probably the greatest complaint that medical claims processors have, considering there are over 30,000 of these codes and they vary by practice—a psychiatrist will have different codes than an opthamologist.

These 5-digit codes (ICD-9's for diagnoses and CPT-4's for procedures) need to be "deciphered" and filled in on the claims forms without exception. If a code is misnumbered or left off by accident, the clearing house will reject the claim and send it back to you.

If you are filling out claims by hand, you will need to obtain code reference books, based on specialty, to look up and use on your form. This can be very time consuming.

If you are using a computer, every software program will let you input codes into a database. This one-time entry will take some prep work at the start, but once you've entered them in, you won't have to worry about them again.

Or better yet, all of these codes are available as software that can be instantly entered and used with your electronic claims program—the full procedure or diagnosis is automatically typed out when you enter the code.

Filing the Form

When you have completed a claim form, you then need to send it to a clearing house. Clearing houses ensure the data is entered correctly and approve the claim for payment by sending it on to the insurance agency. Or, if there is any missing or incorrect information the clearing house will reject the claim and send it back to you for correction.

There are two ways to handle the filing of claims forms if you are entering them in on computer. The first is to print out the form on paper and mail it in to the clearing house—just as you would a handwritten or typed claim. Doing this adds the time it takes to reach the clearing house, and the return postal time if the claim is rejected. This can take up to 4 days for sending and over a month if the claim is denied.

The second way is to directly transmit your claims to the clearing house electronically using a modem hooked up to your computer. This process is called EMC (Electronic Media Claims) and involves sending the form over the telephone line. Electronic claims take priority over paper claims and are processed by clearing houses more quickly than paper claims. Insurance carriers actively encourage providers to use their electronic claims facilities because it saves time, money and confusion.

Medicare also promotes the use of electronic claims because EMC lowers their processing costs—and most carriers pass these savings along in the form of earlier payments. You are also notified of any errors or rejected claims with 48 hours; it is expected that within the next five to ten years, electronic claims filing will be required.

Auditing What's Wrong

When you feel comfortable with your level of medical claims experience, you may wish to pursue a career on the other side of the healthcare arena—aiding the patient by finding billing mistakes and inaccuracies. This type of business is called Medical Bill Auditing and involves a good deal of detective work to help you solve the mysteries of wrongful billing.

The healthcare industry is by no means perfect, and as you can see from the medical claims sections, mistakes can happen—if information is missing from a claim the claim is rejected. But what happens if the information is not correct, i.e., procedure codes were recorded for tests that weren't performed, drugs were charged but never administered, or hospital visits never occurred? The medical claims clearing house will generally not know what the specifics of the procedures and diagnoses are, they will only spot coding or data problems.

For example, say your client goes in to see their physician for an annual checkup. This is a common procedure that is usually covered by the insurance company, but in some instances there might be a co-payment involved.

The exam goes well and your client leaves.

Two weeks later a bill arrives for $625 dollars and a demand for payment. Even though your client made a $10 co-payment (which normally covers the entire exam), there are single line items that say:

Exam	$150
Tests	$125
In-office procedure	$300
Medication	$50
Total Due	$625

What happened? Well, that's what this job is all about—figuring out what went wrong. The first step would be to verify that the name and social security number on the bill match your client. A single letter or numeral can sometimes wreak havoc on the billing process. Next, make sure that the insurance carrier number is correct—if they couldn't find your client, then they won't be covering the costs. Ask the client if their insurance payments are current or if they are still covered by the listed carrier.

If those steps don't uncover anything, contact the billing agency and ask for an itemized and explanatory list of the bill. Ask your client if there were any tests performed other than the standard blood or urine composites. Did the doctor "operate" in any way? Was a procedure involved? What about medication? Were any pills, ointments, liquids or powders administered?

As you can see, this is a business of playing detective— a regular whodunit? And you will see that 9 times out of 10, the billing or insurance agency has made the mistake— which translates to profit for you.

Expanding Your Claims Business

As we've mentioned, once you're comfortable and running your medical claims operation, you can expand in a number of ways that will increase your profits and the ability of your company to handle a variety of tasks.

If you are filing claims for a provider, or providers, turning your business into a full-service management company is the next logical step. You, in essence, take over all functions of the accounting for the provider. Everything from payroll and tax filing, to patient billing and collections. To expand in this direction will require some degree of accounting background on your part, or you can hire someone with this experience to perform those tasks. Either way, you've probably just doubled your yearly income.

Another area for expansion is incorporating your ability to consult or train others. Every task that your business performs can be taught to others for a fee. Seminars that train for next year's insurance changes can mean big business. Or one-on-one consulting to show in-house medical claims people shortcuts and techniques to save money.

If you are reviewing, or auditing medical bills for consumers, advancing into other service invoice auditing is a natural step. Phone bills, electric bills, water bills, gas bills and even cable bills can run amuck and overcharge a great number of customers. By providing full-service utility and medical bill auditing, you can realize even greater percentages in the mistakes you find and the refunds you get back.

There will undoubtedly be numerous other opportunities to expand your business that will become apparent as you go along. No matter how you end up succeeding, succeed you will!

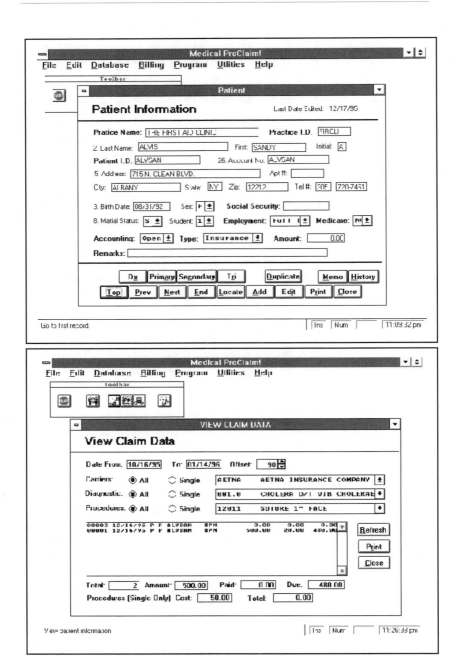

17

Personnel: Hiring Employees

There will come a time when you find you simply cannot do everything by yourself. You will need to consider hiring an employee to help you. It is important to remember that while your profit margin will be higher if you do it all alone, when business reaches the point where you are not able to handle all the functions you need accomplished, it's time to get help.

You can begin by getting someone part time. That person may be interested in working full-time when the need arises. You can play that by ear. In the meantime, you know that for a certain number of hours per day or per week, someone else will be there to do those things you are simply too busy to get to. The idea is to keep the customer happy, and if keeping the customer happy means hiring another person, that's what you do.

When the time comes for you to hire an employee or two for your business, you will want to find the most suitable people you can find. It is important to know what you are looking for in terms of personnel before you start the recruiting and interviewing process, to save time and energy.

> *Knowledge is of two kinds. We know a subject ourselves or we know where we can find information on it.*
>
> **Samuel Johnson**

Selecting Candidates

Have interested applicants fill out a standard employment application (as shown on the following pages) and provide references from former employers and business associates. Do not just take the information provided at face value; check these references very carefully to find out about the applicant's sense of loyalty, responsibility and honesty. This can be done by phone or with a letter.

In either case, request answers to specific questions dealing with those factors that are most important to your job requirements; in this case promptness, character and courtesy, dependability, work habits and loyalty. Be wary of candidates who list friends or relatives as references; they could be trying to conceal unfavorable information.

Employment Application

The Janson Co.
34659 Virginia Road
Anytown, USA 94635

Please Print

As an equal opportunity employer, our company policy as well as federal, state, and city laws, prohibits discrimination in employment based on race, color, religion, sex, national origin, age, or physical handicaps unrelated to job performance.

General

NAME	Last	First	Middle	SOCIAL SECURITY NUMBER

PRESENT ADDRESS	Street	City	State	Zip	TELEPHONE NUMBER	EMERGENCY NO.

PREVIOUS ADDRESS	Street	City	State	Zip	LENGTH OF TIME AT ADDRESS

POSITION DESIRED

SCHEDULE PREFERRED
FULL-TIME ☐   PART-TIME ☐

Are you related to anyone employed by this company?
YES ☐   NO ☐

REFERRED BY

Name _____

DATE AVAILABLE

Relationship _____

SALARY DESIRED
$

Position _____

Employment History   (Most Recent Employer First)

EMPLOYMENT	NAME AND ADDRESS OF EMPLOYER	POSITION/RESPONSIBILITIES
FROM		
TO	SUPERVISOR TELEPHONE NO.	
SALARY	REASON FOR LEAVING	
FROM		
TO	SUPERVISOR TELEPHONE NO.	
SALARY	REASON FOR LEAVING	
FROM		
TO	SUPERVISOR TELEPHONE NO.	
SALARY	REASON FOR LEAVING	

Employment Application

Education

	NAME AND ADDRESS	NO. OF YEARS	YEAR GRAD.	SUBJECTS STUDIED
HIGH SCHOOL				
TRADE OR BUSINESS SCHOOL				
COLLEGE OR UNIVERSITY				
OTHER				

FOREIGN LANGUAGES SPOKEN

References (List the names of three persons not related to you.)

NAME & ADDRESS	JOB TITLE	YRS. KNOWN	TELEPHONE

Skills (Check the applicable areas in which you have experience.)

☐ TYPING
WORDS PER MINUTE _____
☐ WORD PROCESSING   ☐ SPREADSHEET   ☐ EPBX, PBX
☐ DATA PROCESSING   ☐ 10-KEY ADDING MACH. ☐ DICTAPHONE

LIST APPLICABLE   WORD PROCESSING _____   SPREADSHEET _____
SOFTWARE PACKAGES: DATA PROCESSING _____   GRAPHIC _____

CHECK COMPUTER SYSTEMS WITH   ☐ IBM   ☐ MACINTOSH
WHICH YOU'RE EXPERIENCED: ☐ IBM-COMPATIBLES ☐ OTHER _____

LIST OTHER SKILLS YOU POSSESS: _____

Additional Information

HAVE YOU EVER SERVED IN THE UNITED STATES ARMED FORCES?   ☐ NO ☐ YES
If yes, give years of service and final rank:

HAVE YOU EVER BEEN CONVICTED OF A FELONY OR A MISDEMEANOR?   ☐ NO ☐ YES
If yes, explain in detail:

I certify that all information provided on this application is correct to the best of my knowledge. I understand that willful omission or deliberate falsification of this information is grounds for termination.

APPLICANT'S SIGNATURE: _____   DATE: _____

Sample Follow-Up Letter

The Janson Co.
34659 Virginia Road
Anytown USA 94635

Joan Anderson
Staffing & Employment Department
34659 Virginia Road
Anytown, USA 94635

Dear Applicant:

Thank you for applying for a position with the Janson Co. We
welcome your interest in our organization.

We continually evaluate candidates' backgrounds and interests
against our current personnel requirements. Be assured we'll review
your experience and you'll be notified within 10 working days if
your qualifications appear to meet our current needs. If there is not a
current match, your application will be kept in our files and reviewed
as future openings occur.

Again, thank you for your interest in the Janson Co.

Sincerely,

Joan Anderson
Staffing Administrator

The Interview Process

Schedule a personal interview to make your own determination based on poise, appearance, level of interest in the job, abilities and future goals. Write out any questions you may have ahead of time to help you stay on track.

Set up the interview in a comfortable place to put the candidate at ease. For example, if you operate out of your home, arrange to meet at a convenient location during a slow time, or if you have an office, set it up when you won't be bombarded by phone calls or people stopping in. In addition to finding out about their capabilities and goals, you will want to use this time to talk about the company, your expectations, standards and, of course, the pay structure. In this case you might also want to devise a simple test related to the candidate's knowledge of the job.

On-the-Job Training

When you find someone who seems to have all the qualifications needed, arrange to train them on the job. Many owners like to do this themselves, to ensure that their standards are instilled from the beginning and to get a first-hand idea of the new recruit's work habits.

Training may take several weeks or months, depending on the worker's previous experience. Basically, a good training process should involve the following steps:

- Gain the recruit's confidence by putting him or her at ease.
- Find out what he or she already knows.
- Explain and show each step patiently.
- Be sure each step is understood before moving on to another.
- Encourage and welcome questions.

- Have the recruit try to do the task.
- Correct mistakes gently.
- Have him or her repeat the steps to you.
- When you are both comfortable, let the recruit go out alone.
- Review performance periodically.
- Offer support by letting the employee train others when ready.

Taking time to train properly reduces turnover, improves the quality of work performed and in addition lowers your cost of labor.

Overtraining the Ambitious

Sometimes, it is possible to train someone so well they feel they can start their own business in competition with yours. This occasionally happens when an employee realizes you are making money off their hard work. There are several ways to stay on top of your employees' activity.

If you're certain an employee is thinking of starting their own business, take him or her aside and explain the administrative aspects of the business. Find out if they truly realize what you are doing for them in terms of finding work on a continual basis and if they understand how much is involved in running their own business.

In rare cases, you are going to lose an employee who feels confident enough to start their own business and there isn't too much you can do about it.

The Benefits of Happy Employees

Personnel management is a time-consuming job for business owners. However, paying attention to the needs of your employees and working to gain their trust and maintain loyalty can do nothing but benefit your business.

The attitude of your employees about your management techniques plays an important part in building and maintaining your reputation in the community.

If employees are treated fairly and with respect, their job satisfaction will be reflected in the way they do their job.

This is something that can truly keep you ahead of the competition; a loyal, efficient and enthusiastic group of workers is one of your most effective forms of public relations, so never scrimp when it comes to keeping your employees happy. A few important rules of thumb in dealing with employees include the following:

• Never expect an employee to do something that you wouldn't do.   This is why training new recruits yourself is such a good idea; it shows them that you are willing and able to step in and do anything required if necessary.

• Listen to your employees and incorporate their ideas whenever it is feasible. Suggestions that work for the good of the company should be rewarded with a bonus.

• Take the time to talk about business standards and practices so that everyone knows exactly what is expected of them. Outline duties and responsibilities on the job and schedule regular reviews to ensure that they are constantly met. If you find it necessary to talk to an employee about their work habits, do it in private so they are not embarrassed in front of their peers. And do not criticize; merely offer constructive ways that they can improve their performance.

• Treat each employee as an individual. When someone seems to be having personal problems that are interfering with their ability to work, be willing to allow them time off without penalty to take care of the situation. An employee plagued with problems may carry them into the client's home or to the event site and this would have a negative effect. It is much better to get someone to fill in until the regular employee is operating at full efficiency again.

• If a particular client is having a personality conflict with an employee, assure the employee that it isn't their fault and point out the benefits to everyone involved of sending in a replacement.

18

ADVERTISING YOUR BUSINESS

More than 150 years ago, Thomas Macaulay, a British historian and statesman, said, "Advertising is to business what steam is to industry. (They provide) the same propelling power."

Few in business would argue with Macaulay's observation—it is as true today as it was when steam was the driving force behind industry. But the question remains, "How do you get the most out of your advertising dollar?" The answer is to: a) know your customer, b) target your market and c) understand the basics of advertising.

This section discusses the various aspects of advertising, including how to use circulation figures to figure your cost per thousand (CPM) and how to create ads that will bring results.

What Is Advertising?

Advertising informs the public about:

- Who you are,

- What kind of business you operate,

- How they can buy your products or services, and

- Why they should come to you.

Before you even open the doors of your business, you should start thinking about your advertising program— how much money you can afford to spend, where your dollars will be best spent and how to structure your campaign.

Decide what kind of results you expect. Are you looking for immediate sales or ongoing recognition? What kind of customers are you hoping to attract? Are you emphasizing price, service, workmanship or something unique? Once you have answered these questions, your decision as to the best type of advertising for the allotted dollars will be easier to make.

There are three basic types of advertising that you will be most interested in during the first few years of your business.

Start-up advertising: This includes your business cards and stationery, the flyers and brochures you have created to announce your new business, and your initial newspaper advertising campaign. Your main focus here will be on telling people where you are located and what you can offer them.

Ongoing advertising: Once the business is "up and running," so to speak, it will be vital to your success to institute a regular advertising campaign that is well-planned and, this is the key, consistent. Your goal, at this point, is to attract new clients, obtain repeat business from existing clients, and enhance your reputation.

Looking good: After you have reached the point where your business is on steady ground and showing increased profits every year, you can afford to dabble in "institution-al advertising," as it is called in the trade. This is where you pick up the tab to send a dozen kids to the rodeo when it comes to town or sponsor a float in the local Fourth of July parade and, in return, get your name listed on the program or on a banner in the parade. This is primarily name recognition only and, while every little bit is helpful, by the time you can afford it, you probably will be in pretty good shape anyway.

Yellow Pages

Few successful operators claim that they can build their businesses strictly by word-of-mouth referrals. If you're planning to structure a full-scale operation, placing a listing in the Yellow Pages is an absolute necessity.

This requires installing a business telephone, which is equally important if starting the business from home. Calling for service and having a child, for example, answer the phone will kill any interest a potential client may have.

Check with the Yellow Page Directory Advertising Representative of the telephone company to find out when the directory in your area is published. Since they come out at different times during the year depending on the region, it may be necessary to develop a supplemental newspaper advertising or other promotional campaign.

If, for example, you are planning to open for business in August and the phone book in your area comes out in March, you do not want to lose eight months of valuable exposure to prospective clients by doing nothing during that period of time.

Direct Mail

Another way to target specific markets is through direct mail using brochures, flyers, and other materials outlining your medical claims business and detailing the benefits of using your operation. These days direct mail is a more expensive proposition because of postage, but if you mail only to select groups or zip codes within your city to pull the best response, it can be worthwhile.

Mailing lists, broken down by zip codes, income brackets and other specific factors, can be purchased inexpensively from some printers, even small print shops in your city, advertising agencies, local publications and mailing list brokers, all of which are listed in the Yellow Pages.

If you do institute a direct mail program, be sure to send regular announcements to those who've responded to ads in the past but didn't buy your goods or use your service.

Circumstances frequently change, and sending reminders that you are still in business offering quality service at a fair price is sure to result in response at some point.

Just be aware that the average return for direct mail is between 2% and 5% and don't expect the phone to ring off the hook every time you send a mailing. Consistency is the important factor here.

Specialty Items

Specialty advertising serves as an effective reminder. Specialty advertising refers to the matches, pens, key chains and similar items that have a company's name printed on them . . . every time you use the item, you think about the firm, even if it is subconscious.

Investigate the kind of items you can have printed by visiting a specialty advertising representative (listed in the telephone book under "Advertising"). Notepads, pens, pencils, and desk calendars are among your best forms of specialty advertising.

Classified Ads

Don't underestimate the power of classified ads. Many major corporations utilize the classifieds even though they have sizable budgets available for display advertising.

There are several reasons for this:

1) The classifieds are an extremely reliable testing ground for new products, services, and ideas. Although it's true that people who typically "read" the classifieds are a different group from those who scan display ads, they are considered to be responsive and, therefore, can give you a very good idea of whether or not you have placed your ad in the appropriate publication.

2) A short, well-written classified placed in the right publication and under the proper category can be a low-cost method of advertising that guarantees solid returns.

3) If a company is trying to establish a mailing list, a classified ad that features an "Inquiry" statement such as "Send name & address for free details (or a brochure)" is a good way to build up a file of qualified buyers' names. And they can be considered qualified buyers because it takes time, energy and the cost of a postage stamp for them to get your free information. By writing to you they have stated their interest.

4) Classified ads are inexpensive, ranging from 50 cents to $15 per word, depending on the publication. With careful planning, you should be able to get broad-based coverage without putting a dent in your operating capital.

Display Advertising

As with all types of advertising, it is important to define your market when getting ready to place a display ad. Your main goal should be to select a publication that will reach the audience you want and then create a specific ad that appeals to that target group.

To Write or Not to Write?

Writing display ad copy is not for the inexperienced. Although it is possible to learn how to put ideas and words together that will get the results you desire, it is recommended that you hire a copywriter if you have any qualms about producing an ad.

However, if you are confident that you can develop your own ad, remember that it must generate interest through the use of carefully planned words and design.

When planning your ad, keep the following elements in mind:

a) *Visibility*. Your ad may well be surrounded by many others, so make sure it immediately attracts the reader's attention.

b) *Boldness*. Use large art and/or a bold headline as a focal point.

c) *Simplicity*. Don't overwhelm the reader with too many fine details. The ad's main point is lost and so is the reader's attention. This is particularly true in a small ad.

d) *White space*. Just because you have, say, a 4 x 6 inch space to work with, it isn't necessary to fill it up with graphics. White space is a necessary component in assuring your ad will be read.

e) *Use legible typestyles*. The easiest to read are Times Roman and Bookman (the type used in this business guide), which are known as serif typefaces because of the tiny strokes at the tops and bottoms of the letters. San serif (without strokes) type such as Helvetica are okay for ads containing few words, but are difficult for the eye to follow when there is a lot of text. Also, be sure that the type is large enough—generally nothing smaller than 10 point type should be used.

> *Advertising is the greatest art form of the 20th Century.*
>
> *Marshall McLuhan*

Design and Typesetting

It isn't necessary to be a great artist to create an ad, especially these days with the availability of impressive graphic materials, including cut-out and transfer (press-on) letters in different type faces, symbols, borders and design ideas through graphic art supply companies, such as Formatt and Chartpak. Also, most word processors contain computer graphics that can really dress up your ad at a low cost.

If you feel uncomfortable about laying out your ad so it has eye appeal, consider hiring an art student to handle the job for a prearranged fee or as a school assignment (talk with the head of the art department to see if they have a work/study for credit program). Just be sure to review the student's work prior to making a commitment.

Also, check with the advertising department of the newspaper or magazine you are planning to advertise in. There may be graphic artists or designers on staff who will work on the layout for you. In fact, there still are newspapers in the country that offer full services, from ad concept to design work, at minimal charge to clients.

Publications work on tight deadlines so be sure you start the process early enough to get a proof copy of your ad back in time to make any corrections. You can imagine the frustration of seeing your ad appear with the wrong address. Although the publication would probably do a "make-good" for you and run a corrected ad at no charge, the damage has already been done. The final responsibility for the ad rests on you, so plan ahead.

Tracking Ad Response

Some customers will tell you that they saw your ad and might even let you know what they liked or disliked about it. They will probably be in the minority, however, so you must develop methods for determining if your advertising is working for you.

One very simple way is to include a coupon for something in the ad and to count the number of coupons you get within a certain test period after the ad runs. There is one major problem with this, however. Even the most well-intentioned people often cut coupons, file them away in a "safe" place and totally forget about them.

So, although you will be able to gauge response to some degree, be aware that many of the people who come into or call your business have probably seen the coupon, but simply mislaid it or are not the kind of folks who use them.

Predicting Response

There is a standardized formula in advertising which provides a barometer for predicting how much response can be expected from either a display or classified ad. The formula states that you will see 1/2 of the total responses from an ad within a certain period of time after receiving your first inquiry or order. For an ad to run in a daily newspaper, the period of time is 3 days; for a weekly newspaper or magazine, it is 6 days; the period is roughly 15 days for a monthly publication, and within 25 days when running in a bi-monthly. Although there are exceptions, this provides a base from which to track response.

Determining Your Cost per Thousand (CPM)

The CPM equation helps you develop a cost-effective campaign. Basically, it tells you what your ad cost per 1,000 readers will be.

Most publications will provide a CPM comparison upon request (some include it in their media kits), but you can easily figure it out for yourself with just a few facts from publications you are exploring as advertising vehicles.

For convenience sake, CPM equations are typically based on the rate of a full-page black and white ad. You simply divide the full-page rate by the thousands of the overall circulation. It's important that you get the circulation, not the readership, as magazines and newspapers typically claim that their readership is 2 to 50 percent higher because of "pass-along" of the publication to friends.

For example, if a certain newspaper is charging $2,000 for a full-page ad and they claim their true circulation is 200,000, you will be paying $10 per 1,000 readers for your ad space. Another specialized publication's full-page rate may be $1,000 with a circulation of 50,000. The cost per 1,000 readers will be much higher— $20 per 1,000, but it might be worth it if, for example, you have a unique product or service that is geared to an exclusive market.

Benefits of Paid Circulation

It is also important to know that publications with a paid circulation generally have a readership that is more inclined to respond to advertising. This is because of the simple fact that they are a captive audience who have taken the time to order the publication. This is especially valuable if you ever have a product or service that you're planning to market through mail order.

You can find circulation, readership demographics, advertising rates and other important information about a number of publications (especially those with national distribution) through Standard Rate and Data (SR&D) or the Ayer Directory of Publications (and their monthly updates), available through the research desk at your local library.

Recently, the Advertising Research Foundation and the Association of Business Publishers conducted a study to determine the impact of advertising on the sale of products.

Several different products were used for the study and each was advertised for a 12-month period in an appropriate publication. The results were interesting, but not surprising to anyone who has ever utilized a solid advertising campaign in promoting their business.

- More advertising meant more sales.

- Determining results from an ad campaign generally took 4 to 6 months. (One or two insertions does not indicate viable results.)

- Color in advertisements dramatically increased response and sales.

- A well-developed ad campaign kept on working for a year and sometimes even longer in publications with a high "keep" appeal.

Knowledge and belief in your service, faith in yourself and respect for your customers are the keys to successfully building your future. As you go about starting up and establishing your business, remember the word "profit." This alone should give you the necessary motivation to get out there and confidently tell the world what you have to offer.

Promotion and Public Relations

Informing the public about your business through the use of business cards, brochures, mailing pieces, and specialty items such as desk calendars, pens, and note pads imprinted with your company name, is a form of advertising that is known as promotion.

The things you can do over and above your paid advertising and promotion that help build your image and keep your business in the public consciousness are referred to as public relations. It is a fine line in terminology, but can make or break your business if not addressed.

There are many clever ways to extend the effectiveness of your advertising and promotional dollars, as illustrated in the following examples.

A Little Creativity Goes a Long Way

The owner of a pet grooming business leaves a business card and a brochure featuring a 20% discount coupon everywhere he goes. When he is running errands, he always takes a handful of brochures with him to hand to store clerks, gas station attendants and waitpersons he runs into along the way.

> *Advertisements contain only the truths to be relied on in a newspaper.*
>
> *Thomas Jefferson*

If he sees a car with a dog in it, or one with a bumper sticker announcing the owner's affection for their pet, he slips a brochure under the windshield wiper. Does it work? Absolutely. He claims that 45% of his new business is from the recipients of his handouts and the majority of them become regular customers.

Another business owner who operates a small walking tour service in her beachside town sends out a one-page quarterly newsletter featuring historical and other facts about the area to everyone who has ever taken the tour. She includes a $10 coupon which can be redeemed by former clients or their guests.

She states that many of her clients are local residents who send their out-of-town visitors on her walking tour, simply because she makes sure they are aware that she is still in business and generates enthusiasm through the newsletter.

Charity Tie-Ins

Other ideas you might consider include promoting humanitarian outreach. For example, for every ten referrals to your service, you donate a predetermined amount of money to a local charity. You can easily keep track of their purchases by punching a hole at the edge of a card designed by you or your printer strictly for that purpose.

When you are ready to present the check to the particular charity, make sure the chairperson of the organization is going to be available to accept it and be sure to contact the local press and invite them to the "event." In most cases, they will give you free coverage.

Reminder Cards

Sending regular "thinking-of-you" cards to your past and present clientele is especially effective with service businesses. Again, it assures the customer that you are friendly, reliable and successful—a real plus for your credibility.

Networking

Check out local business-owners groups and the chamber of commerce in your area. Pay your membership dues and join as many as possible. Membership offers you the opportunity to meet people who might use your service, and will, at bare minimum, tell others about you once they know you, feel comfortable and understand what you are offering. You will also be given a listing in the group's directory, generally under your specific category. And, as is so often the case, the members are prone to supporting others involved with their group. It is quite possible that members with compatible businesses will put a stack of your cards or brochures on their counter or in their referral file. In return, you may be able to promote their businesses to your customers. This is the true meaning of "networking."

> *The advertisement is one of the most interesting and difficult of modern literary forms.*
>
> *Aldous Huxley*

The directory also gives you bonafide access to an instant mailing list, which you can use to send out promotional flyers or brochures. Participating in their events and the willingness, for example, to speak at functions about your area of specialization will let people know that you are community-minded. This involvement will work to project a positive image for you and your business.

Customer Service

One of the most overlooked areas in promoting business is the impression we create when dealing with customers. The ageless philosophy that the customer comes first and is always right has, it seems, gotten lost in the shuffle in these days of fast-paced, fast-buck dealings from Main Street to Wall Street.

As a small business owner, it is guaranteed that customers will flock to you if you make them feel important. It is as easy as greeting them warmly (instruct your employees, if you have them, to do the same), maintaining a courteous attitude and inviting them to come back soon—even if they have not used your services.

Word travels fast and if you create an atmosphere that makes each and every person you deal with feel like the only person in the world, you can be sure they will tell their friends and neighbors.

Free Publicity

Free publicity also comes under the category of public relations. This includes articles and interviews in newspapers and magazines or coverage on radio and television, featuring interesting or unusual facts about you and your business.

As any newspaper reporter or talk show host will tell you, everybody has a story to tell. The key is to get the media to zero in on yours and make it available to the public. If you have trouble deciding on a unique angle for your story, invite several friends over for a brainstorming session to create a newsworthy item.

Use your imagination to explore the creative possibilities of your business venture. And then look at your personal story. Perhaps you have completely switched fields with your new business. That represents a story angled toward risk-taking. Maybe you have successfully turned a hobby into a business venture, or created a unique product or developed a new twist on an old theme.

These all qualify as human interest stories. Newspaper and magazine editors love them—almost as much as their readers enjoy them.

Once you have your story angle, call the managing editor or the feature editor of the newspaper. Give him or her a brief description of who you are and what business you are in. Tell them you will be sending out a press release and would be happy to arrange an interview at their convenience.

Invite them to visit your place of business and get a firsthand look at what you are doing and how you're doing it. Do the same with program directors or talk show hosts at regional television and radio stations, offering your availability.

If, on the first attempt, your presentation fails to result in an article, follow up in three to six months, possibly with a new story angle. In the meantime, however, send out regular press releases announcing new developments with your business—the grand opening, special events, details on your business philosophy, extra services and features. Even if they don't run a full story on you alone, there is a good likelihood they will include you in a feature story about local entrepreneurs or people in similar businesses.

An Effective Ad Campaign

All of the methods outlined above, along with others you will develop, keep your name in the consumer's mind. The effectiveness of an advertising/publicity campaign can be measured by conducting a simple marketing survey with new customers. Make it standard practice to ask them where they heard about you and your business.

Keep a tally of the responses in a notebook. A periodic review will give you hints of where to allocate future advertising funds. If, for example, the majority of your customers are being drawn from your direct mailings to potential clients, keep them going on a steady basis. The same principle applies to Yellow Pages display ads, specialty ads or word-of-mouth advertising.

The justification for investing in advertising and promotion is time. If you attempted to contact all of the people who read ads and press release material in newspapers or those who listen to talk shows, you would never have time to conduct your business . . . you would be too busy recruiting.

It can't be stressed enough: Time is money. As a small business owner, you will want to devote as much attention as possible to the production end of your venture and let your advertising and promotion work to bring in the customers.

19

RESOURCES

Associations

American Association for Medical Transcription, 800-982-2182

Books

The AAMT Book of Style for Medical Transcription, Claudia Tessier, CAE, CMT, RRA, 1994 AAMT, 800-982-2182

American Medical Association Manual of Style, 8th ed., Williams & Wilkins, 1989, ISBN: 0-683-04351-X

The Chicago Manual of Style: The Essential Guide for Writers, Editors and Publishers. 14th ed. The University of Chicago Press. Chicago: The University of Chicago Press, 1993. ISBN 0-226-10389-7

Dictation Therapy for Doctors, George Heymont, Galen Press, Ltd., 800-442-5369

The Elements of Style. Shertzer, Margaret D. Collier Books, Macmillan Publishing Co., New York, 1986. ISBN 0-02-015440-2.

Getting Business to Come to You, Edwards, 800-847-5515

The Gregg Reference Manual, 7th ed. Sabin, William A. Glencoe/McGraw-Hill, New York, 1992. ISBN 0-02-819922-7 (spiral-bound text ed.).

Harbrace College Handbook. Hodges, John C., and Mary E. Whitten. Harcourt, Brace & World, Inc., New York, 1967. ISBN 0-15-531810-1.

Health Service Business On Your Home-Based PC, by Richard Benzel, 800-233-1128

The Independent Medical Transcriptionist, Donna Avila-Weil, CMT, and Mary Glaccum, CMT, Rayve Publications, 800-852-4890

Medical Transcription Guide: Do's and Dont's, Fordney, Marilyn Takahashi, and Marcy Otis Diehl. W.B. Saunders Co., Philadelphia, 1990. ISBN 0-7216-3798-1.

The MLA Style Manual., Achert, Walter S., and Joseph Gibaldi. The Modern Language Association of America, New York, 1985. ISBN 0-87352-136-6.

The New York Times Manual of Style: A Desk Book of Guidelines for Writers and Editors, Jordan, Lewis (ed.). Times Books, New York, 1976. ISBN 0-8129-6316-4 (paper).

Saunders Manual of Medical Transcription, W.B. Saunders Company, 800-545-2522

Working as a Medical Transcriptionist at Home (Report) MT Monthly, 800-951-5559

Periodicals

At-Home Professions, 2001 Lowe Street, Fort Collins, CO 80525, (303) 225-6300

California College for Health Sciences, 222 West 24th Street, National City, CA 91950, (800) 221-7374

Health Professions Institute, P.O. Box 801, Modesto, CA 95353, (209) 551-2112

Journal of the American Association for Medical Transcription, 800-982-2182

MediSoft Corporation, (800) 333-4747

MT Monthly, 800-951-5559

PC & Mac Connection, Computer Hardware (Mail Order) Computers, software, modems & printers, (800) 800-1111

PC & Mac Zone, Computers, software, modems & printers, (800) 248-0800

San Antonio Reporting Institute, 5430 Fredericksburg Rd., Suite #300, San Antonio, TX 78229, (800) 638-9281.

Schools/Home Study Programs, AAMA, 20 N. Wacker Dr. #1575, Chicago, IL 60606, (800) 228-2262

Software

Dolby Systems, (800) 878-7828

Doctor's Office Medical Billing Software, H.J. Morgan Inc., (305) 663-1219

Martel Electronics, 2013 Miraloma Ave., Placentia, CA 92670, (800) 553-5536

Mavis Beacon Teaches Typing, Mindscape Software Available through MacWarehouse, (800) 255-6227

MediSoft Patient Accounting–Just Claims, MediSoft Corporation, (800) 333-4747

Transcription Equipment, Briggs Products, 7887 University Blvd., Des Moines, IA 50306, (800) 247-2343

Small Business Associations & Government Agencies

American Marketing Association, 250 South Wacker Drive, Chicago, IL, 60606-5819 (Marketing publications available to non-members.)

Bureau of the Census, Washington, DC, 20233. (Statistical data)

Copyright Office, Library of Congress, 101 Independence Avenue SE, Washington, DC 20559 (Information on copyrighting written and visual materials.)

Council of Better Business Bureaus, 4200 Wilson Blvd.Suite 800, Arlington, VA. 22203 (Ask for a listing of their "Booklets on Wise Buying.")

Dun & Bradstreet, 299 Park Avenue, New York, NY, 10171. (Send for the booklet "This is Dun & Bradstreet," an overview of publications and services.)

International Franchise Association, 1350 New York Avenue NW, Suite 900, Washington, DC, 20005. (Regulation and information on franchises.)

Minority Business Development Agency, Office of Public Affairs, Department of Commerce, Washington, DC 20230

National Association for the Self-Employed, P.O. Box 612067, DFW Airport, Fort Worth, TX, 75261-2067.

National Association of Women Business Owners, 600 South Federal Street, Chicago, IL, 60605.

National Federation of Independent Business, 150 West 20th Avenue, San Mateo, CA, 94403.

National Insurance Consumers Organization, P.O. Box 3243, Merryfield, VA 22116-3243. (Send self-addressed stamped envelope for free booklet, "Buyer's Guide to Insurance.")

National Minority Business Council, Inc., 235 East 42 St., New York, NY 10017 (Quarterly newsletter for small & minority business.)

National Small Business United, 1155 15th Street NW Suite 910, Washington, DC, 20005. (Send for info on federal legislation for small businesses.)

National Trade and Professional Associations of the United States. Available through the Research Desk at your local library.

Occupational Safety & Health Administration (OSHA), Department of Labor, Washington, DC 20210. (Employment regulations.)

Office of Information and Public Affairs, U.S. Department of Labor, 200 Constitution Ave NW, Washington, DC, 20210 (Request publications list regarding employment.)

Small Business Administration, 1441 L Street NW, Washington, DC, 20416. (For booklets and information on the Service Corps of Retired Executives—SCORE.)

INDEX